Piano + Music Theory:

Start Playing The Piano, Songwriting & Reading Music Theory Right Away. Lessons For Beginners Or Refreshing The Advanced Via This Book + Diagrams, Charts & Bonus Videos

Discover "How to Find Your Sound"

http://musicprod.ontrapages.com/

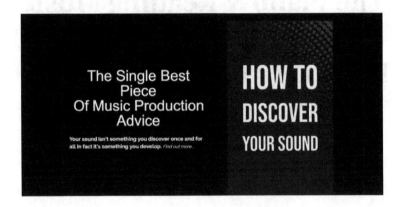

The Single Best Piece Of Music Production Advice

Your sound isn't something you discover once and for all in fact it's something you develop. *Find out more...*

HOW TO DISCOVER YOUR SOUND

Swindali music coaching/Skype lessons.

Email djswindali@gmail.com for info and pricing

Piano Lessons

Cut Out The Fluff, Start Playing The Piano & Reading Music Theory Right Away. For Beginners or Refreshing the Advanced Via This Book & Bonus Videos

Table of Contents

Introduction

The piano is a beautiful and soulful musical instrument that most people are fascinated by. A lot of people aspire to learn to play the piano for this reason. However, learning the piano can be a tad difficult unless you are taught well. Traditionally, such lessons tended to be boring. A lot of beginners get frustrated when they see slow progress despite their efforts. Learning from a tutor is an ideal scenario, but not everyone has the financial backup to spend on private tuition from a certified teacher. That is where self-learning comes into the picture. Learning online or reading a how-to guide is one of the best ways, second only to a real instructor.

There are scores of piano books on the market, but a lot of them tend to be uninspiring and a little difficult to follow, especially for beginners. Most piano books have random techniques and songs that are of no real help at all to the reader. That is where this book comes in as an engaging and informative guide to learning the piano. The chapters in this book are put together in a simple format following a step-by-step method.

As you go through the videos and book in this course, you will find it much easier to learn how to play the piano like an expert. It is a complete learning experience and is delivered with helpful videos with guidance from a piano teacher. If you are someone who has always wanted to learn the piano or just someone who wants to improve on their skills, this book and the videos are just what you need.

You don't have to waste your time on unhelpful books or courses anymore. Instead of spending a lot of hard-earned money on private lessons or useless books, you'll learn a lot more here at a fraction of the cost. The videos in this course will allow you to feel as though a teacher is present in the room with you. But the added advantage is that you get to set the pace as you learn. Although you will have to put in some regular effort, the joy of playing the piano will make it worth it. If you learn the theory and practice all the techniques and exercises mentioned, you will be able to play everything from the simplest to more complex musical pieces. If you go through the lessons in the book, you will see that every lesson builds on the last, and the videos help you learn everything necessary.

Like anything new, you have to put in time and effort to be able to play the piano well.

An important aspect of learning to play the piano or any other musical instrument is cultivating the right attitude. If you have a happy mindset, your mind and body will be able to learn a lot better. You need to be positive and believe that your efforts will pay off, which will help speed up your progress. Approach your piano practice as an exciting activity for the day.

Good practice habits are also crucial for playing the piano. Be regular in practicing all the exercises mentioned here and watch the videos for hands-on guidance. If you put in the time, although you will start with simple musical pieces, soon you'll be able to play your favorite songs regardless of how complex they might seem to a beginner. You will see rapid progress if you have good practice habits, but you need to be proactive about it. Practice every day if possible, and aim to practice well in the time you put in. It is not about practicing for hours but focused practice for at least 30 minutes a day. Avoid missing out on this regular practice even if you are busy. Be patient and think long term.

Once you learn how to play the piano well, you can enjoy playing music for the rest of your life. Piano playing helps give a new perspective on a lot of things in life and also improves your concentration, determination, and self-confidence. If this is what you want, you need to stop wasting your time and money on other unhelpful piano courses. This book and the bonus videos provided would be all you need. If you have difficulty accessing the videos please email me at djswindali@gmail.com

So start reading, and you will soon be on your way to playing the piano effortlessly.

Part One: Introduction

Chapter One: How Books and Videos Work

As you start reading this book, you will learn everything about the piano that you possibly need to know. The piano is a beautiful instrument that gives us amazing music. However, it is not just about banging on some keys with your fingers. There is a lot of practice that goes into the making of a proficient piano player. As we have mentioned before, this book aims to guide anyone who wants to learn to play the piano the right way. It is unlike other books and lessons that fail to give students a strong foundation before playing the piano. The lessons in this book will help you learn the following amongst a lot more:

● What the piano is and its origins

● Music theory

● Fundamentals of playing the piano

● Basic terms associated with the piano

● How to avoid beginner mistakes

● Strategies to play better

● The right way to practice

You will learn all this and more in this book. The video that goes along with this book will help to guide you through the process in a way that makes it feel that you are attending a real lesson. The difference is that this lesson will be a lot better than most others that are not half as efficient. Make sure that you go through each of the chapters to make the most out of this book.

Once you put it all to practice, you will be on your way to becoming an excellent piano player.

Chapter Two: Essential Music Theory

About Music Theory

So what is music theory? It is the study that enables you to understand music, the practice of music, and its possibilities. It involves guidelines and practices that are used to identify the various methods through which sound can be used to express emotions. Music theory can help you to translate any musical composition into terms that are intelligible and familiar. This helps to enhance your confidence in creating and performing music. It also improves your ability to communicate with musicians other than yourself. You must acknowledge the importance of learning music theory to enhance creativity and develop a keen sense of music. Although it may prove challenging, understanding how music operates can help make the process of producing music much easier. The main purpose of learning music theory is to develop the capacity to compare different pieces of music and relate the similarities or differences between them.

The following are some essential terms in music theory:

● Notes

● Intervals

● Harmony

● Scales

● Rhythm

● Melody

Notes

Notes refer to symbols that are used to denote musical sounds. A musical note will represent the pitch and duration of any specific sound in musical notation. It will also represent what class the pitch belongs to. A note is the most minimal element used to characterize musical sounds. When the strings of the piano vibrate, some molecules are set into motion in the air surrounding the string. This vibration in the air tends to occur at a frequency that is equal to the strings' vibrations. The human ear captures the vibrations and processes it in the brain. The brain usually attributes specific notes or sounds to specific vibrations. This is why musical notes are considered the building blocks for creating any musical chord or melody. The length of a note is linked to the duration of that note. The vertical position represents the pitch.

Letters are usually used to identify musical notes since it makes them easier to write and read. This kind of notation is used universally and thus allows musicians from any country, speaking any language to communicate effortlessly when it comes to music.

Most of the time, in western music, there are 12 notes in an octave, and they can be integrated into many ways to create good music. You can work on seven basic notes at any time, and these are A, B, C, D, E, F, and G. Any of these seven notes can be modified so that they sound different from their usual sound. To do this, the pitch can be increased or decreased to make the note "flat" or "sharp." Sharp notes are denoted by "#" while flat notes are denoted by "b." Your notes can be written as D#, Eb, Gb, etc. You will also see that they can be written a little differently again. For instance, D# can also be written as Eb, while C# can be written as Db. They are enharmonic notes, and they are written according to the key that they belong to. The sharps and flats are the symbols that come after the letters or accidentals.

Twelve notes make up an octave and also form a chromatic scale. You will notice that certain notes have different names even though they sound the same. For instance, an A sharp note will sound the same as a B flat note. It can seem confusing at first, but you soon get the hang of it.

In the piano, the white portion is used to layout the main notes, including A, B, C, D, E, F, and G. If you want to make a specific note flat, just move down a single key on the left. To make that same key sharp, you would have to move a single key on the right. This is a system called "moving in half steps."

The black keys have two names and two functions. If you notice the first black key that has a set of two with a circle around them, it is either a C sharp note or a D flat note. C is the white key on the piano, and if you start playing from there, you have to move down one on the left to make it flat or move down one on the right to make it sharp. However, if you play from the white D key, you would have to move one key on the left to make it a flat note. If you read this again, it will seem less confusing than it does at first.

The 12 musical notes on the keyboard of a piano are as follows:

● A

● A#/Bb

● B

- C

- C#/Db

- D

- D#/Eb

- E

- F

- F#/Gb

- G

- G#/Ab

Musical Scales

You will learn more about scales later in the book. Scales are a group of tones that belong together and may also belong to some key. Scales usually consist of more notes that are not played simultaneously, and this is how it is different from chords.

Musical Intervals

Intervals are an important part of musical structures, and this is why they are essential in ear training. The distance between the pitch of two different tones is an interval. Numerical values and their quality represent intervals. The number of tones in diatonic scales is the numerical value. Every interval will have a sound and name for itself.

When the interval between two notes is large, the difference between their pitches will also be large. If the interval between two notes is small, the difference in the pitches will also be small. To understand an interval, you have to consider three parts:

● The distance of the interval

● Harmonic or melodic quality of the interval

● Quality or type of interval

Whole Steps and Half Steps

But first, you have to understand more about half steps and whole steps. Half steps and Whole steps are like building blocks for intervals and musical scales. If different half steps are combined with whole steps, you get many different types of musical scales. A half step is the smallest interval that is used in western music. Half steps are also called semitones, as they are the next lower or higher note. For example, when you move from C to C sharp or from E to F.

Half step intervals are of two types: chromatic half steps and diatonic half steps.

1. Chromatic Half steps are also called chromatic semitones. Here the half step interval will have two notes with similar letter names. For example, C to C sharp note is a chromatic half step. There are twelve different notes on a chromatic scale, and every note is a one-half step higher than the note before it.

2. Diatonic Half Steps are also called diatonic semitones. Here the half step interval comprises two notes with different letter names. For example, a C note to D note is a diatonic half step.

Chromatic half steps and diatonic half steps are the same actual notes and are enharmonic equivalents. Semitones are half steps or half of a tone. Accordingly, a whole step describes the interval of two semitones. Half steps and whole steps are used in music for many different reasons. One of these reasons is to create musical scales. The other reason is to work out intervals.

The Distance of the Interval

Numerals are used to describe intervals depending on the number of letter names from the musical alphabet existing between the notes. For example, if you consider the notes C and D, the difference between the number of letter names is two. Thus the interval is of a second. When the difference is three notes letter, the interval would be a third. If the difference between notes were six-letter notes, then the interval would be of sixth and so on.

Octave

While playing notes from C to C, the note is an eight-letter note and interval is eight. This interval is called octave or 8ve. Since it is eight notes higher, this interval is called an octave.

A Unison Interval

Intervals can be on different as well as the same notes. For example, the same note from a piece of music can be played by two different instruments. This kind of interval is called Unison. The notes are written next to each other while writing a harmonic unison interval.

Quality or Type of Intervals

Describing different types or quality of intervals is the next step. For instance, C to Eb has a difference of three letters, and so the interval is of the third. However, the interval is also a third between C to an E note. The difference between such intervals is the quality of the interval.

Types of Musical Interval Quality

Here are the five unique types of intervals:

● Perfect intervals

● Minor intervals

● Augmented intervals

● Diminished intervals

● Major intervals

You have to understand that all the notes in a major musical scale are a perfect interval or a major interval.

Perfect Intervals

Three different types of intervals can be called perfect intervals. These include a perfect 4th, perfect 5th, and perfect 8ve. The interval will be perfect if the highest note is in the same major scale as that of the lowest note. When the interval of 4th, 5th, or 8ve is not on the major scale, it will not be a perfect interval. As an example, C to F sharp would not be a perfect interval despite being a fourth because the C note is not in the same major scale as the F sharp note. Instead, it is an augmented interval of fourth.

Major Intervals

Major intervals within a major scale include a major 2nd, major 3rd, major 6th, and major 7th. If the upper note of an interval is within the major scale other than that of the lower note, it will be a major interval as long as it is not a 4th, 5th, or 8ve. The specific number of intervals can be worked out by using lower notes as the first number, and by counting the letter notes to the upper note. If the upper note is in the major scale of the lower note, it will either be a perfect interval or a major interval. It is a perfect interval if the interval is a 4th, 5th, or 8ve. If the interval number is different, it is a major interval.

Minor Intervals

If all the major intervals mentioned above are made smaller by a single half step, you get a minor interval. For example, consider C to E, which is a major third, and then turn the E into an Eb, making it a minor third. Similar to major intervals, there are four possible minor intervals: a minor 2nd, 3rd, 6th, and 7th.

Augmented Intervals

Intervals become augmented when major or perfect intervals are extended by a single half step without changing the letter name. So if you take F to G and turn the G into a G sharp, the interval is only increased by a half step. Thus a major second turns into an augmented second. Augmented intervals are very similar to perfect intervals.

Diminished Intervals

If you make any of the perfect intervals, unison, 4th, 5th, or 8ve flat, they become diminished intervals and not minor intervals. For example, A to D note is a perfect 4th, but if you turn the D into a flat note, it becomes a finished D.

If a half step flattens a minor interval, it becomes diminished. For example, E to D is a minor 7th, but you can make it a diminished 7th by making the D a flat note.

You get a diminished interval when a half step flattens a perfect interval. If a half step flattens a minor interval, it also becomes a diminished interval. You also get a diminished interval by making a major interval flat by a whole step.

Harmonic and Melodic Intervals

Intervals can be categorized according to interval numbers, interval quality, and also as harmonic or melodic intervals. However, the harmonic and melodic intervals are not the same thing as harmonic or melodic minor scales. Harmonic intervals are how two concurrently played notes are described. It is called a harmonic interval to show that the notes were played in harmony. When two notes are played one after the other, it is called a melodic interval. The melodic interval shows that tones are part of the melody.

Compound Intervals

If an interval exceeds twelve semitones or the perfect octave, a compound interval occurs. The 9th, 11th, and 13th are also included. In music genres such as the blues or jazz, it is common to see these three being utilized. In the interval of an octave and a 2nd, it is a 9th. In the interval of an octave and a 3rd, it is a 10th. In the interval of an octave and a 4th, it is an 11th and so on. This is how compound intervals are named and formed.

Consonant Interval and Dissonant Interval

If a particular combination of music produces a pleasing sound, it is a consonance interval. You can easily find many examples of this phenomenon occurring. For example, when you play major and minor thirds together if the fourths and fifths are perfect and also when music is being played in unison. Dissonance is the opposite of consonance. Here you get harsh sounds from the combination of music. For instance, dissonant intervals include minor and major sevenths. In general, consonant intervals are regarded as the perfect unison, major and minor third, etc. It is considered a perfect interval when the harmonic relationship between the tones is also present in the natural overtone series. However, some other basic intervals are considered imperfect. The dissonance concept is usually perceived in the context of music.

Video: Essential Music Theory For Piano

To access the supporting video please visit the following link:

https://youtu.be/oqgKyJQAJE0

In this supporting video Sorn Buranadham reveals some essential terms in music theory that piano players need to know. This relates to the previous chapter. Discover the twelve notes on the piano and how to denote musical sounds. You will also discover musical intervals which are an important part of musical structures, and why they are essential in ear training. Watch and watch again. If you don't have a piano you can still practice these exercises using a table or piano mobile application and following the video. Enjoy.

If you have difficulty accessing the videos please email me at djswindali@gmail.com

Chapter Three: The Piano, It's Notes and Keys

On the modern piano, there are a total of 88 keys where 52 are white, and 36 are black. It includes a minor third with seven octaves. The black keys are raised and set a little back from the white keys. Every key on the piano keyboard signifies a specific note. The white keys signify the seven names of the notes while the black keys signify if the note is sharp or flat.

The black keys on the piano will always be in a consecutive group of two, followed by three. One simple trick is to think of the two black keys set as a pair of chopsticks while the set of three will be like the tines of a fork. Chopsticks begin with C and forks start with F. This will help you identify the white keys on the keyboard. On the left of the two black keys or chopsticks is the C note. On the left of the three black keys or the fork is the F note. Once you go up from the note C, you get D, E, F, and G. At G, and you have to go back to the beginning of the alphabet. You will see that this alphabet pattern is repeated continuously in octave groupings. These octave groupings are groups of eight white keys with black keys in between.

As you know now, all seven note names A, B, C, D, E, F, G are on the white keys of the keyboard. Black keys represent the musical notes. These black keys are given the same name as the white key that is closest to them, but they have a suffix added to them. If a black key lies on the right of a white key, it is sharp. If a black key lies on the left of a white key, it is flat. Since every black key lies in between two white keys, they have two names depending on which white key you approach from. For example, the back key on the right of C is a C sharp note, but it is also a D flat note.

The key helps to identify a tonal center for a song. This center is a note around which the whole song will revolve. All the notes in the song or musical piece will gravitate towards this base note. For instance, if a song is in the C key, every note will gravitate towards C.

The following are possible keys in music:

- Key of C

- Key of Db/C#

- Key of D

- Key of E

- Key of F

- Key of Gb/ Key of F#

- Key of G

- Key of Ab

- Key of A

- Key of Bb

- Key of B/ Key of Cb

History of the Piano

The piano is probably one of the most well-known musical instruments in the world, and it does not need an introduction. You can hear the music from a piano being played in music from many different genres and from many countries. Even if you don't play the piano yourself, you probably know what the instrument is at the very least. However, this book will cover everything that you need to know about the piano.

The piano is a musical instrument with a large keyboard in a wooden case that encloses metal strings and a soundboard. When the piano keys are depressed, the metal strings and soundboard are struck by hammers. Once the keys are released, the vibration of the strings will be stopped by dampers. Two or three pedals are used for regulating the length and volume. The interaction between the strings and hammers is what helps produces harmonious music from a piano. The large keyboard on the piano is a long row of keys that are pressed down on in a particular order to play a particular piece of music. The sound is not produced directly by the strings. Once the keys are pressed, the hammers strike the strings, and these cause vibrations. The vibrations are then transmitted to the soundboard that is connected to the strings via a bridge. The soundboard amplifies the sound from the strings, and it also modifies the resulting tone.

An Italian named Bartolomeo Cristofori invented the piano around the early 1700s in the city of Florence. The exact year of the invention of the piano is yet to be determined. The instrument has initially named the pianoforte. The term piano was coined from this initial name. The name pianoforte was derived from the Italian words fortepiano and gravicembalo col piano e forte. Fortepiano comes together from two words - piano and forte. These words are found in the sentence gravicembalo col piano e forte, which means a harpsichord with soft and loud. Piano means soft, and forte means loud. If the keys in the piano are pressed heavily, the strings will be hit by the hammers heavily as well, and the sound produced will be heavy and loud. If the keys in the piano are pressed softly, the strings are struck softly by the hammers, and the sound produced will be more soft and subtle.

The structure of the piano is unique and is unlike any other instrument used to play music. Most of the earlier versions of the piano had entirely wooden frames. However, modern pianos tend to have a cast-iron frame. The wooden frames could not withstand as much tension generated from the strings as the cast iron frames can. This means that the modern-day pianos are much sturdier, and pianists can play on them more vigorously. The sound on the modern pianos is also much louder than that from the older pianos.

In the modern version of a piano, there are 88 keys and a keyboard with seven full octaves. There are also a couple of extra keys to the modern piano. Bartolomeo Cristofori is given credit as the inventor of the piano. Still, he was not the first person to have created a musical device that utilized the same keyboard striking actions. This kind of musical instrument already existed around the 15th century. Cristofori only built further on that concept and helped advance the principles to the point of near perfection. To this day, pianos are still built based on the model of Cristofori's piano.

Around the mid-18th century, the piano started gaining popularity. People began manufacturing it in many different forms and styles. German manufacturers adapted the lighter version of the piano, and this was also much cheaper than other versions. This lighter version of the piano was called the square piano. Famous musicians such as Amadeus Mozart and Muzio Clementi started composing their pieces on this square piano. Their initial pieces helped in developing a distinct style of piano composition and playing. The success of these musicians helped establish the piano as an elite musical instrument. The piano started being linked to chamber music, salon music, concerti, and other musical performances that the elite preferred.

Upright pianos became popular around the 1860s, and the German-made square piano started going out of favor. The upright piano has a design that was similar to that of upright harpsichords. The strings extended upwards from the keyboard in both. This is why pianos were now built to be tall despite efforts to make them look as elegant as possible. The extreme height of these upright pianos still posed a problem, and John Isaac Hawkins recognized this. He then went on to lower the piano strings to the floor to make the piano look much better suited for smaller rooms and elegant homes.

In the following century, there were a lot of innovations being made on the piano. The initial 16 tons string tension rose to 30 tons. This change helped in allowing newer pianos to sustain and hold tones in a previously unknown spectrum. Around the mid-20th century, there was a lot of advancement in the field of technology, and this allowed electric pianos to be built. The new electric versions of the piano could generate tones that created a sound that was never heard from the traditional versions of the instrument. In an electric piano, the sound generated by the player was passed through an amplifier and then through a loudspeaker.

Facts About the Piano

From what you have read earlier, you know the piano is a huge contribution to both modern and classical music. This was first created in the year 1700s and has changed in shape and size over the years. Now, we have synthesizers, grand pianos, and digital pianos. We will look at these in detail later in the book. Before we dive into learning the basics of playing the piano, let us look at some facts:

● The piano was called the pianoforte since you could play notes both loudly (forte) and quietly (piano). Before the piano, there was an instrument called a harpsichord that only played soft music.

● The piano has 12,000 parts in total, and 10,000 of those parts are moving. This is an instrument with many small pieces that must work perfectly together, so you get the sound you want.

● You need 230 strings if you want the piano to have its full sound range. These strings are made of steel and produce sound when the hammers inside the piano hit the string. Every string holds a tension of 170 pounds, and it is for this reason you need a specialist to tune a piano.

● A piano is both a percussion and a string instrument. People believe it is a percussion instrument since the hammers inside the piano strike it to make the sound.

● A piano has the range of an orchestra.

● The keys were made out of ivory until the 1940s, and it is for this reason people call the keys 'ivories.' They are now only made of plastic.

● Ever wonder what the pedals are used for? The pedal on the right is often used and is the sustain pedal. The pedal in the middle, called the sostenuto pedal, will sustain notes that you press. The pedal on the left, called the damper pedal, will soften the sound.

Without further ado, it's time to learn more about the instrument and how to play it.

Part Two: Progressing from Beginner to Advanced Chords

Chapter Four: First Steps

Types of Pianos

When it comes to choosing a piano, many different types are ranging from the hybrid to the grand piano. At first, pianos could only be classified as the grand piano or the upright piano. However, there are a few more added to the list these days. As you read on, you will learn more about each type of piano, and it will help you decide on the piano for yourself.

Grand Piano

The frame of the grand piano is horizontal, and thus the strings on this type of piano are also horizontal. The strings go in the opposite direction of the keyboard in the grand piano. This type of piano is the most recognizable and tends to be displayed quite often in movies or used in concerts. The action of this piano is beneath its strings. Using gravity, it goes back to a resting state after the strings are struck. Out of all other pianos, you get the richest sound from the grand piano. The longer the piano is, the better and richer the sounds it produces. Grand pianos are usually used for concerts and such. Under the grand piano, you have six more types to choose from. The six types of grand pianos include the baby grand, the concert grand, the medium grand, the petite grand, the semi-concert grand, and the parlor grand. The semi-concert grand is often called the ballroom grand because it was usually used in ballrooms.

Upright Piano

The upright piano is also called the vertical piano. This design of the piano was developed to make the piano more compact and accessible in homes. While the grand piano has horizontal strings, the upright piano has strings that are extended vertically. Here the hammers work horizontally, but the springs are utilized to return to the initial resting position. These upright pianos have a further classification depending on their size. Upright grand pianos are the ones that are very tall with extremely long strings. It is commonly seen in homes, music schools, churches, etc.

Electric, Electronic and the Digital Piano

As technology advanced in the early half of the 20th century, pianos of this category were invented. Electric pianos were invented first and released in 1929. After the electric piano came electronic pianos in the 1970s. Digital pianos were invented around the 1980s.

Originally, the electric piano had metal strings with a magnetic pickup, loudspeaker, and also an amplifier for generating and producing sound. These metal strings were later switched to metal tines. The magnetic pickups were switched to electromagnetic pickups. A keyboard amplifier was used to amplify the generated sound. Effects units are used to manipulate sounds as well. For musicians who played rock, funk, or jazz-fusion, the electric piano was the chosen instrument. It was also preferred by people who wanted to start learning how to play the piano. It was very rare for this type of piano to be seen in any concerts or other performances.

On the other hand, there were no acoustic pieces in electronic pianos. This meant that there were no tines, hammers, strings, bridges, etc. Instead, it included a synthesizer that utilized oscillators and filters to create a sound that is similar to the one produced by a piano. Electronic pianos are used widely to learn and rehearse music. An advantage of these pianos is that you can connect headphones and use them in private settings. A synthesizer and speaker are used in these pianos to generate sound. They may be inbuilt or otherwise.

Soon after the invention of electronic pianos, digital pianos were invented as well. Digital pianos do not have acoustic parts attached. They rely on digital sampling technology, which is a type of sound technology that generates piano-like music. You have to use an amplifier and speaker to generate sound with this type of piano. These could be inbuilt or otherwise. You can also use headphones to practice privately. Some other advantages of digital pianos are sustain pedals, MIDI interfaces, a variety of piano voices, and others. The MIDI interfaces allow you to connect the piano to any other tools or instruments for added effect. Sounds produced on the digital piano can be recorded as well, so you can play them later. Computer software can be used to modify these sounds.

Hybrid Pianos

A hybrid piano is an acoustic grand or an upright piano with added electronic features. These are real pianos but have electronic enhancements. Hybrid pianos made an appearance around the early 2000s and are loved by many because they can be used for recording as well as for playing in performances.

Specialized Pianos

As the name suggests, specialized pianos are not exactly like your typical piano. Many such specialized pianos were created over recent years. This includes the mini piano with long metal rods for striking the hammers. Another example is the prepared piano that has added elements placed within it to alter the sounds produced by the piano in some way or another. Other examples include the toy piano and the player piano.

Regardless of what genre of music you play, the chords remain the same in all of them. What may change is your tempo, articulation, expression, and other aspects, but the chords remain constant. No matter what genre of music you play, a C major seven chord will contain the same notes and have the same quality. This is why it is essential to have a thorough knowledge of chords while you learn the piano. It works as a good center point, even when anything else changes or shifts.

The chords that you play have to complement the melody that you are playing. If not, the sounds produced will not be pleasing to hear or appreciated by any audience. The chord progression is important to play chords for melodies. Chord tones lie within these chord progressions. These are chords that are pleasing to the ear, as they sound good together. It is crucial to learn about chords in-depth if you want to be a good pianist. This will allow you to please any audience with harmonious and sweet music. Learn the chord theory as well as possible and practice regularly. Hone your skills as you learn as much as you can about piano playing. Choose the type of piano you want, depending on your skill, purpose, genre, etc.

Learning How to Play the Piano

If you go to a regular piano lesson, you will experience the following method of learning. They will make you rehearse the scales until your fingers become flexible. You will be asked to practice this for as long as you can so that your skills improve. Most teachers will make you do the Hanon series exercises. You can then pick a piece of music and start reading it slowly. At first, you can read and slowly start playing with both hands as you read. This way, you can keep practicing until you get adept at it. You will be made to practice until you can achieve the required speed for that particular piece of music. Metronomes are usually recommended to help speed up the process. After an hour or two of practicing, you will be tired and want to play around for a while. Most of your lessons will proceed in the same way as you learn each piece by heart and practice playing them until you can do so well. The problem is that this kind of lesson is not the right way to go about learning the piano. You will not make progress beyond the intermediate level if you follow such lessons. All you will be doing is practicing some pieces of music until you learn them by heart. You will not learn any useful techniques that can help you when you get stuck, either. The lesson plan mentioned above is one that just tells students to keep practicing and learning musical pieces until they learn them by heart. It does not help the student learn how to play the instrument; this task is left to themselves. This is why many mistakes are bound to happen, and the music will probably sound flat while playing. As you learn the methods taught here and utilize them, you will notice the difference in learning.

Many students quit piano lessons when they see how slow they are or because of a lack of progress. It is impractical to expect instant results from a few lessons, but any smart student will realize that the type of lesson mentioned above is not worth their time. In such lessons, you just end up learning from intuition. The teacher is not laying out any helpful techniques or methods that you need to learn. This means that your time and money spent on such lessons were for naught. Such teachers tend to use this intuitive approach for teaching because they were not accustomed to the right methods that help them to develop an intuitive approach. However, every piano player must learn the right lessons so they can play the piano in the best way possible.

Finger Positions

You need to learn how to position your fingers the right way on the piano. To do this, you have to practice regularly. First, relax your fingers and place your hand on some flat surface so that your fingertips rest on it. Your wrists should be at a level with your knuckles. Position your hand and fingers in the shape of a dome and keep your fingers curved. The nails of your thumbs should be parallel to the other fingers when you view them from above. This bending of your thumb will be useful while playing chords with wide spans. It helps to position the tips of your thumbs parallel to the case, and this prevents you from hitting adjacent keys. It also helps to position the thumbs such that you use the right muscles for raising and lowering the thumb.

Your fingers will be positioned in a way that they curve down slightly and are curled while hitting the surface at a 45-degree angle. This curled position will help the fingers keep playing actively between all the black keys. With the tip of your thumb and the other fingertips, form a semi-circle. If you do this with both your hands side by side, both the thumbnails will face each other. When you play the piano, make sure that you only use the part of the thumb that is right beneath the thumbnails and not the joint that is between the middle and nail phalanges. If you play with the tips of your thumbs, it helps to ensure optimal uniformity since it is already quite short. The phalange is close to the fingertips of your other fingers. The front pad of your fingertips should be hitting the keys because that flesh is much thicker than the fingertip.

You should start easing into this practice. Whenever you feel that you have to stretch your fingers while playing, just straighten them. However, this will depend on what piece of music you play. Every beginner has to master and follow the curled position in strict compliance while playing musical pieces because it has its perks.

The Distance From the Piano and Bench Height

The bench height for every piano player will be determined according to what suits them best. The same applies to the distance that they sit away from the piano as well. You have to determine the right distance and bench height yourself.

To begin with, you should sit on the piano bench, so you have your elbows by your sides. Your forearms should be perpendicular to the piano. As you place your hands on the piano keys and get ready to play, your elbows should be a little below the height of your hands. This means that your elbows will be at around the same height as the keys.

The distance between your bench or yourself and the piano should be enough to allow your elbows to miss your body slightly. Your hands should be on the piano keys in this position. Don't sit in the middle of the bench and instead position yourself a little closer to the front edge of it. This will allow you to place your feet properly on the pedals or the floor. You should always pay close attention to the bench height and the exact location of the bench. It makes a lot of difference when you are playing the chords. To help you test this posture, play any two black keys as loudly as you can at the same time. For a louder percussive sound, you should tilt slightly forward and then press down hard on the keys using the entire weight of your shoulders and arms. You also have to make sure that your shoulders are completely engaged while doing this. If you want to produce loud and pleasing sounds while playing, you have to keep your shoulders and entire body completely engaged. Use the maximum force possible and don't just depend on your hands and forearms while playing. Your sitting posture and bench height are appropriate when you can produce such sounds comfortably. You should get a bench that has alterable height so that you can adjust the height to be able to play using your finger pads. Most fixed height benches are at least a higher and will make you play with your fingertips.

Listening and Analysis While Starting a Piece

To kick off the process of learning a new piece of music, listening to a performance or recording it is the best way. Some people believe that listening to the piece first is akin to cheating. The disadvantage of listening first is that you would rather imitate what you hear instead of being creative while playing. Imitating is quite difficult because each person has a unique playing style. It can hinder the learning process for a beginner when they compare their playing to what they heard a professional play. It may cause them to believe that they lack the talent to be a skilled piano player. You have to understand that you don't need to be able to copy someone else's playing style, in the same way, to be considered a good player. However, listening is beneficial because it helps you when you want to try playing any new and unfamiliar piece of music. Listening to recordings is as important as you are practicing your finger techniques.

After listening to the musical piece, you have to analyze the configuration of it next. It will help you determine your practice routine and how much time you may need to be able to master that piece. Time estimation is crucial when you try to achieve a practice routine for a new piece. For instance, if you want to play Fur Elise by Beethoven. The first part of the analysis will be numbering all the bars on the score. The bars may not be marked so you can do so by using a pencil to mark every tenth bar right above the center. Any part of the beginning should be counted as bar 1. If you count it as a full bar, it becomes difficult to recognize the first partial bar. In this piece by Beethoven, half of the piece is learned just by playing the first four full bars and then repeating them fifteen times. You get 10 bars because 6 bars are replayed four times. It allows you to learn nearly 70% of the piece within half an hour. While repeating these bars, you will observe two difficult interruptions. If you have a year or two of experience in playing the piano, you can learn 50 bars of this musical piece within the week. You will be able to play the entire piece within two weeks. Certain tricks help you to achieve such skills and get past any tough passages. Understanding these tricks will help you get better at playing different pieces.

The Hard Parts Should Always be Rehearsed First

You should start by practicing the more difficult sections of the piece. It takes more time to learn these difficult parts in a piece, so dedicate more energy to them first. Then you can get through the easier sections much quicker. You will soon learn that most pieces end with the difficult parts. So when you learn a new piece, start with the end.

Practice Speed and Velocity

You don't have to worry about playing the piano too fast. It will only stress you out and cause you to make more mistakes while playing. Trying to play fast as a beginner will also cause you to acquire bad habits while playing. You shouldn't try to increase your speed by forcing your fingers to play faster. Instead, you have to find better ways to increase your speed, like in a parallel play. It is much easier to play faster with parallel play. You should try coming up with better hand positions or motions that will help increase your speed. This is something that you will learn more about in this book. Certain techniques such as relaxation, thumb over method, etc. will help you achieve this speed. The post-practice movement is also quite important. When you don't see any obvious progress after a few minutes of doing something, it means that you are doing something wrong. At this point, you should switch to something new that will help you see progress. When a student uses the intuitive method to learn a piece, they keep repeating the same thing for hours on end and see very little improvement. If you want to be able to learn musical pieces in less time, you have to take a different approach. You will see your technique improve when you play at a certain speed that you are comfortable with while playing precisely.

When you play with both hands together, it also helps your technique and speed get better. It is usually easier to play with hands separately than with both together. Playing with both hands can be more stressful, especially for a beginner. You will not improve faster if you try playing as fast as possible because it will just stress you out and cause more mistakes while playing. While playing hands separately is easier, it is eventually quite confusing because you have to gain speed and be more accurate while playing. One solution to this problem is changing your speed of play quite often. When you are practicing a hard passage that is above your skill level, you can bring up your speed slowly as you keep practicing. You can make things easier by trying faster speeds and determining what has to be changed so that you can play faster. Later you can reduce your speed again and try those changes to help increase your speed. When you want to change your speed of playing, first try playing accurately at the fastest speed that you can. Then try playing even faster and try to notice what has to be changed. At this point, you needn't worry about accurate playing too much because it will get better with more practice. Use all the new motions that you can come up with to improve the playing at a better speed. It gets a lot easier at this point. Try keeping up with this increased speed but then play slower so that you can be more precise and relaxed. This exercise helps to increase your playing speed, and you also get to practice your skills a lot more. It may seem difficult to achieve a certain speed at first, but anyone can do it with some practice.

Relaxing

When you are trying to get up to speed while practicing a piece, it is very important to relax. When you relax, it allows you to use the muscles that you need to while playing. Being stressed will cause you to use more muscles and energy than you need. Relaxing will allow you to work hard without being tense. Relaxation has two schools of thought. In one, it is stressed that with time, it is better not to practice rather than engaging in practice with a lot of tension. Here you learn how to relax and play single notes. You will be advancing quite carefully, and they only give you material that you can play without any tension. In the second school of thought, they believe that relaxation is important for acquiring skills but should not be given too much thought. However, this approach is only better is you are aware of its other side.

When you perform any action, your brain keeps working hard regardless of how small the task is. If your brain is unconditioned, it will exert more power for the most menial tasks. If some task proves to be more difficult, the brain seems to confine the entire body in a mass of tensed muscles. Relaxation is very important in this kind of scenario. This is why you have to consciously and deliberately make an effort to ensure that the brain muscle is not tired through unimportant tasks. However, this proves to be a little difficult since it goes against the natural principle of how the brain usually works. You have to practice relaxation as much as you practice playing the keys on the piano.

When you think of relaxation, it does not mean that you have to relax all the muscles in your body. Relaxation while playing means that you only use the ones necessary for playing, and the others are allowed to be resting. It is a skill that you have to practice a lot to master. To learn how to relax, you should start with easy musical pieces and practice relaxation alongside. One way of doing this is by practicing a parallel set and increasing the speed until you start feeling stressed again. At this point, you should practice how to relax. To do this, you have to find some arm movements that will allow you to relax and let go of the stress while you continue to play with your hands. Some beginners stop certain basic functions in their bodies, such as swallowing or breathing while trying to concentrate more. It is important to learn how to relax while maintaining such basic functions in the body. When you manage to do this, it makes you feel more like a professional in the field. You have to relax in a way that you can concentrate on playing while allowing your body to conduct its normal functioning. It is well known amongst piano learners that the throat tends to feel dry after a practice session. This usually means that you stop swallowing while playing. You have to learn to avoid doing this in the future.

A lot of students are not taught how to relax when they begin learning the piano. These students tend to think that their hands get better at playing in some magical way if they spend hours at practice. However, the hands just get used to following the right motions for relaxing. This is why certain skills are not very difficult to acquire, while others seem to be much harder to get the hang of. This is also why some students pick up on certain skills faster than others. Relaxation is a state in which you will find it easier to play while feeling relaxed. Achieving this state of relaxation is quite natural for some, while it is a lot more difficult for others. If students are taught properly, they can all learn to relax and play in the right manner.

Relaxation is a way to conserve energy and spend only as much as is required. There are two ways in which you can do this. One way is by avoiding the usage of any unnecessary muscles in the body while playing. Another is by letting the muscles rest once you are done using them. The first way is quite easy if you use something like the one-finger gravity drop. Here you just allow gravity to control the drop, and the rest of your body is comfortable as you sit on the bench. It makes playing the piano much easier. However, if the person is tense, they will use muscles even while dropping their hands. In the second manner of conserving energy, you have to learn some techniques to relax every muscle as you reach the end of the key drop. Gravity does the work by pulling your arms down for a gravity drop. However, when your key drop is about to end, you have to create some tension to stop the hand. After this, you can quickly relax your muscles again. You need to avoid leaving your hand or resting in over the piano to prevent pressing down. Your elbow is resting in the air, and the weight of it makes this difficult.

One major cause of tension is stressing opposing muscles. If you are not aware of doing this, you can cause injury due to prolonged stress. It is important to learn how to control opposing muscles independent of themselves. It is also crucial to master how to control each finger of the hand individually. You have to understand that stress puts you in a fight against yourself, and that is a fight you can't win. This is why it is important to keep stress as far away as possible.

Some people tend to turn off muscles due to a lack of training. Usually, you will forget about the muscles when you're done using them. But when you are carrying out fast finger work, there is an imminent need to relax, or your fingers will not get time to rest and prepare for the next note.

There are many effective exercises for practicing relaxation. One of these is to start with a single key down and using the same finger to play a slightly loud note. Then you can apply force on the up and down region to turn it off. Once you turn it off, you have to return to how you felt at the end of the gravity drop. As you carry out this exercise, you will notice how it takes longer to relax when you play harder. Thus you need to work on shortening the time you take to relax. One benefit of these relaxation techniques is that they become a part of you over time. If you give relaxation the required amount of attention, it will help you be relaxed no matter what you are playing. If you go through Chopin's teachings, you will see that relaxation, avoiding unnecessary repetitions, and gravity drop is important topics.

Post Practice Improvement or PPI

In a single practice session, there is only a specific amount of improvement that you can expect. One reason is that there are two ways in which you can improve in the first place.

The first way in which you can improve is by rehearsing and thus mastering all the notes and motions to help you get more skilled. This is applicable for passages that you have learned how to play already. The second way is what we will focus on, and it is posted practice improvement. Post practice improvement occurs due to the psychological changes that tend to occur when you learn some new technique. Such changes take place over a long period at a slow rate because of the need for nerve and muscle growth. When you are practicing, you have to measure your progress continuously. When you feel that you are not making much progress, you have to stop doing what you were doing and do something else instead. You will see that your technique starts improving after an effective practice session. In the next practice session, you will realize that you have improved if you do this right. However, this one-day improvement may not seem very significant. Nonetheless, the total effect of it builds up over time and makes a huge difference.

It is usually considered okay to rehearse different things at the same time so that you can improve at them all simultaneously. However, this may also cause damage to your technique if it causes stress or some bad habits. PPI takes effect only if you practice to a certain extent regularly. You also have to relax so that you can ensure you have carried out enough repetitions for the PPI to work. You don't want your improvement to result from some stressed motions. Relaxation will allow you to do it the right way.

There are a few different types of PPI, and they depend on what holds back a particular individual. One way that post-practice improvement is manifested is in the amount of time it takes for it to be effective. This can vary from a day to many months. Using hand motions or muscles that you haven't yet used can be linked to shorter times. Taking several weeks can be linked to nerve connections like hands together. A longer amount of time will be linked to the growth of the brain, muscle, and nerve cells, as well as the conversions of slow muscle cells to fast muscle cell types.

You have to do everything right if you want the post-practice improvement to work optimally. A lot of students are unaware of some simple rules and nullify the effect of their PPI. These students play even worse on the next day following a practice. Such mistakes usually occur due to the incorrect use of slow and fast practice. If you go through any extra or unnecessary motions or stress during a practice session, it will lead to the development of bad habits instead. One common mistake that nullifies the effect of PPI is that some students play very fast before they stop their practice. What they should be doing right before they quit practice is to follow a moderate pace of playing. The last play tends to have some excessive string PPI effect. You will be learning some ideal methods for post-practice improvement using this book. These are far more helpful since they will stress learning segments that you can't play yet.

Playing hands together slowly and increasing speed over time can be an inefficient method because you don't get enough time for the necessary amount of repetitions this requires. The PPI process becomes a lot more confusing because you will be mixing more easy material with very few more difficult tunes. Your hand motions and speed will also be incorrect. If you take a look at some examples, you will see that post-practice improvement is not a new phenomenon. For instance, take the example of a marathon runner. If the individual is just a beginner, they will find the task of running a mile quite difficult. They will probably be able to push it until half a mile before they need to rest. Then they will have to stop halfway before the finish line again to rest. However, the next day, this same person might be able to complete the mile with a single break in between, and this will be an improvement. This is a post-practice improvement, and this is how most marathon runners condition themselves before running a long marathon.

When it comes to playing the piano, the analogy is that playing too fast can ruin this post-practice improvement. However, playing simpler material can help you to better improve.

PPI Occurs to a Larger Degree During Sleep

During the waking hours of the day, the human body is unable to carry out proper maintenance and growth of any worn out parts. When you sleep, it allows your body to repair itself, and so sleep is not just for resting. However, the sleep required for this should be normal timely sleep that is preferably the REM type. While babies can grow rapidly and over a short period, adults are unable to do so. You need the required amount of sleep if you want to see good post-practice improvement. The best routine to see real improvement is practicing the piano in the evening and reviewing the same once you wake up in the morning. This will allow you to learn and retain better over the long term.

Other Methods for Piano Practice

Slow Play

When you are learning a new piece of music, repetitive slow play can be quite harmful since you don't have any way of knowing if your motions are right or wrong in the beginning. There is a higher possibility of playing the wrong way when you start because there is a nearly uncountable number of ways that allow you to play the wrong way. However, when it comes to playing it right, there is only one way. When the wrong motion is gradually increased in speed, the student will face a speed wall. They are only able to overcome such a speed wall if they manage to learn some new way of playing and unlearn the older wrong way. They will have to keep repeating this sufficiently for a slight increase in speed until they achieve the final speed. This is why slow playing can be a big waste of time for someone learning the piano.

However, once you are aware of the dangers of slow playing, you will be able to implement it at the right time instead. You have to know how to think ahead during slow play. This is because a beginner can easily fall behind the music mentally when they are playing a new piece. This develops into a habit and will reach a point where you have no control over it. Thinking ahead while playing slowly will help you predict any hard notes and also allow you to have enough time for the appropriate action. Try to play pieces at the beat intended. its

Tempo and the Metronome

You have to use a metronome for maintaining speed and beat accuracy to ensure accurate tempo. When you use the metronome, you will find that you are better able to identify the errors you make while playing.

Using One Hand to Teach the Other

If a beginner does not practice their hands separately, they will end up having a stronger right hand compared to their left hand. This usually happens because right-hand passages are easier to play while it takes more energy to play a left-hand passage. This is why the left hand tends to lag in terms of speed as well as technique. So a weak left hand refers to a technical weakness in the left hand. Your better hand is the best teacher when it comes to passages that you can play better with one hand as compared to the other. To teach your weaker hand, you can play the note first with the better hand and repeat the note with the weaker hand. You have to understand that playing the piano is about control and not about muscle power. Some beginners think that they need to achieve a certain amount of muscle strength before they develop a solid technique. A certain amount of endurance is required, but it is more important to find a way to eliminate any stress and increase stamina this way. One way of achieving this is by having shorter practice sessions. For a beginner, practicing for 15-30 minutes initially will be enough. You have to build your stamina for playing and not your muscles. You can do this by practicing pieces that you have already finished or change the music. Practicing breathing exercises and playing with hands separately will also help.

Bad Habits

Bad habits will cause you to lose a lot of time while playing the piano. Most of the bad habits in piano playing are linked to excessive stress. A lot of these bad habits are difficult to determine, and regular practice sessions only can help you with this. Hitting the piano keys loudly is a common bad habit. When a beginner does this, they equate the loudness with their excitement. If you listen to yourself play, you can help correct this bad habit. However, this is easier said than done. It is a common habit for most students to focus entirely on playing, and in the process, they forget to listen. All their attention is on playing music. Most people do not listen to music or the sounds they create. Playing too loudly can create harsh tones, and this is the kind of bad habit you have to avoid or correct. Many other bad piano playing habits can be observed, but the takeaway is that every student needs to put in some correctional behavior to improve rapidly.

Damper Pedal

Another important point is that you should play a new piece without the pedal first with hands separately and then hands together. You can keep doing this until you can play the new piece at the final speed in a comfortable manner. Practicing with the pedal from the beginning can cause a student to become a sloppy player and develop bad habits. It also prevents them from understanding the concept of control and practicing it. The rule to follow is that if the music does not indicate a need for the pedal, don't use it. The pedal should be played the same way that you carefully play the piano keys.

Reducing Difficult Passages

A simple way to reduce the duration of practicing the piano is by selecting shorter sessions. When you look at some tough passage with 10 bars, certain note combinations might confuse you. You don't have to focus on practicing the other notes. Take time to understand and learn the tougher parts first.

Hand, Finger and Body Motions

Hand Motions

If you want to be an ace at playing the piano, you have to master various hand developments. Some of the fundamental ones that you have to remember are pronation and supination, thrust and pull, flick and wrist, claw, and throw movements. These are joined into compounds on most occasions. They usually come as two by two. For the development of fingers, you have to develop muscles in the upper half of the body.

Pronation and Supination

Your hands can revolve around the pivots of the lower arms. Pronation is the interior pivot, and supination is the exterior revolution. In pronation, the flicking finger descends while in supination, the thumb goes upward. These two movements are significant in various instances, like while you play octave tremolos. Hand pivots occur with the radius turning against the ulna. A good way to carry out the flicking finger is speedy pronation. If you want to play the octave tremolo, the flick finger movement is simple, but the little finger has to be moved quite quickly. You have to blend some developments for this. The octave tremolo can be played if you move your little finger with your upper arm and your thumb with your lower arm. This, along with finger movements, will let you play the octave tremolo.

Thrust and Pull

In simple words, thrust is a force or a pushing motion. While playing the piano, it is a driving movement that is accompanied by a little climbing wrist. It is used in playing harmonies. The movement is a comparative one away from the fallboard. In such movements, the vector section that goes down may be smaller or greater than the complete movement while taking some salient controls into account. Pushing is one of the main reasons for the bent finger positions. The force helps to create a softer and smoother submission. This is why you should try various things and include some thrust and force while rehearsing harmonies.

Claw and Throw

When you move your fingertips towards your palm, it is called a claw. When you open your fingers outward into a straight position, it is called a throw. A lot of beginners can't grasp this simple concept and randomly move their fingers. Just like the push and pull movements, these allow more movement with a smaller key drop. Keep this in mind and try out a few different approaches instead of focusing on descending your fingers down for a key drop. Trial and error will allow you to see what works for you and what doesn't. The claw movement is easier and more normal as compared to the throw position. The throw is a mix of hook and toss. You can loosen the key drop movement by pushing your fingers outward but with a smaller claw position.

Flick

One of the most useful movements in playing the piano is the flick. It is a mix of pronation and supination or the invert. It is similar to a snappy pivot with a counter turn of your hand. Nearly all duplicate sets can be played at any speed. During a quick practice session, speed comes into play while interfacing duplicate sets. The flick is a very similar movement to a large placement. It is especially so when it is used in scales and arpeggios. A single flick can be led very swiftly without any pressure, and it adds to the speed of playing later. However, a brisk flick should be restacked because repeated quick flicks can be annoying. Flicks can also be used in playing combinations and then be restacked while playing a parallel set. Movements like the flick do not have to be very big and are usually quite small. This is why they are not always considered a genuine movement and instead are more linked to energy.

Wrist Motion

As we mentioned before, the wrist movement is another important part of playing the piano. It is especially vital when you play with your index finger or thumb. The general rule for wrist movement is that you should raise your wrist for the pinky finger and lower it when you use the thumb. However, it is not a hard and fast rule. You can add wrist movements to pronation and supination to create rotational movements while playing some dull sections like LH backups. Your wrist can be moved in many directions. When you are playing, your lower arm should be in line with the finger you are playing with, and this can be achieved with side-to-side wrist movements. It allows minimal horizontal weight on ligaments that are moving the fingers and thus reduces the chances of injuries such as carpal tunnel syndrome. If you end up playing or always composing with a sideway-positioned wrist, it means that you may face some other inconvenience. As far as complete unwinding is concerned, your free wrist can serve as a pre-imperative.

Body Motions

There are a lot of tutors in experts who give support for using the whole body while playing the piano. However, there have been questions about what this means. People also wonder if there are any specific criteria for when body motions should be used while playing the piano. A lot of research has shown the playing technique depends more on finger and hand movement as well as the ability to relax. It would be impractical to expect the body to remain still when the hands are connected to the body frame. It would be natural for the body to move when you move your hands as well. The body follows the movement of the sides, so when you extend one lower limb, you will also have to extend the other to maintain balance. This is especially relevant when there is no pedal being used. You must understand that every small movement, including that of the fingers, requires signals to be passed along neurons. These neurons are connected to the spinal cord and brain. Every part of the human body is somehow connected and so that it would be natural to expect body movement while playing the piano.

As we have mentioned in another part of the book, relaxation is a very important part of playing the piano well. It is also important in mastering hand and finger movements since a lot of muscles are involved in this. Even though most body movements can be controlled naturally, it is important to give it significance when it comes to piano playing. Some movements are quite obvious, while some are not as obvious as the others. Remember that relaxation also involves breathing freely. If you experience a dry throat after practicing the piano, it signifies uneasiness or tension in the body. During relaxation, you should only be using the muscles that are required for playing, and all other muscles should be rested during that time.

Finger Motions

Before you think of learning any other useful movement, you should also consider separation of the main body frame from your hand's fingers and upper arms. If there is tension in the body, then all the interconnected muscles may result in unexpected mistakes while playing. This is quite significant in HT play coupling and can destroy the flow of two hands. Coupling is one of the main reasons for a mistake while you play the piano. For instance, if you move one hand, it may cause an involuntary movement in your other hand due to the connection between your muscles. This does not mean that you can ignore body de-pairing while carrying out HS practice, but it should be applied intentionally while you do any HS work. Once you master de-pairing, it is quite easy to perform, but physically it involves a lot of coordination. Just like Newton's Law of Motion states, a movement in one hand results in a movement in the other. The human brain is quite complicated and advanced, so it easily allows us to understand what de-pairing means.

This is one reason why you should practice de-pairing. When you learn a new thing, the coupling effect comes into play unless you keep practicing. One of the worst ways in which coupling comes into play is when you learn something difficult while dealing with stress. When you make a stressful and deliberate attempt to try and learn something new, you might also be adding some unnecessary movements. This happens quite often during HT practice, and eventually, it will cause interference when you are playing later. It will affect your ability to master the art of playing the piano and also affect your speed. However, if you keep consistently practicing the right way, it will help you eliminate any such unnecessary movement. Using your upper arm as well as your shoulders, you can play the piano softly or loudly. Any type of playing has its requirements. For instance, if you want to play softly, you need a dependable and constant platform to generate such automated forces from. Your arms and hands have many potential movements that can act as a reliable platform. When they are connected to a steady body, you get a reference platform. You can infer from this that the general precision of an excellent pianist comes from the body and not the fingertips.

Playing the Piano Faster

Now let's talk about ways to rehearse fast scales. Fast movements tend to be like that of a glissando when you are playing quick scales. This type of movement allows you to carry your thumb close to passed fingers since the fingers from the index finger to the pinky finger are somewhat pointing in reverse. You should be able to play a quick octave these lines after a few moments of training. Once you become proficient at it, you should not find long scales more troublesome than the short ones. You should also be able to handle TU the same way as HT. However, many teachers consider it's futile to rehearse HT scales.

Scales

Activities or scales should not be rehashed thoughtlessly. It is important to build up expertise in playing certain scales and arpeggios. This will allow you to master some vital fingerings and methods that are useful in pursuing a routine while playing. You should practice all the scales and arpeggios until you know their fingerings. The sound should not be boisterous, but it should sound definitive and fresh. When someone listens to these tunes, they should instantly feel uplifted. Your goal should be to rehearse until the fingering of every single scale is programmed into your brain and body.

Arpeggios

Being able to play arpeggios properly can be tough, especially for beginners. Arpeggios incorporate broken harmonies along with mixes of short arpeggio sections. For the push and pull movement, we will use Beethoven's Moonlight Sonata, and for the cartwheel movement, we will use Chopin's Fantasie Impromptu. To play arpeggios, the suppleness of hands is a basic requirement, and this is especially so for the wrists. This suppleness has to be joined with everything from the push, pull, glissando, and cartwheel movement to TU or TO. We would also like to mention that the Moonlight Sonata is a little difficult because of the speed it requires. Those who have smaller hands will find it difficult to play this piece compared to those who have a wider reach.

Fast Chromatic Scales

The chromatic scale includes semitone steps. In chromatic scales, the most important aspect is fingering since there are many approaches to fingering them. The standard way to finger is 1313123131345, beginning from C and for climbing RH while it is 1313132131321 for rising LH another octave. It is hard to play this quickly because it comprises the smallest conceivable parallel sets and also contains the biggest conjunctions. A large number of conjunctions are what normally reduce the speed. The advantage is the straightforwardness, and this makes it appropriate for nearly any chromatic fragment. It can begin from any note and is very easy to recall. Another variety is 1212123121234, and this has a little more speed and legato. It is easier for a pianist with big hands to use this.

Memorizing as a Tool

For a pianist, memorizing can be a very beneficial tool. Surprisingly, there are very few people who know of the advantages of memorizing for playing the piano. Once you get better at playing the piano, you will understand how memorizing can be extremely helpful. One reason for this is because a lot of technical skill is required in playing the piano and if you are not efficient in memorizing, it is not possible to be an advanced player. You have to understand that the most difficult passages that you play will also have to be played off by heart. If you don't identify as a memorizer yet, you will need sheet music when you play, but it still just acts as psychological support. You don't need the sheet music to play once you get better at it, but the sheets help with little cues that help with continuity. Most pianists just play musical pieces from hand memory, and that is what you should aspire to do as well. Memorizing is an important part of perfecting any piece of music. If a student is unable to memorize the music that they practice, they are rarely able to surpass the performance of someone who memorizes well. Non-memorizers tend to move on to a new piece even if they haven't perfected the piece they are currently practicing. One reason for this kind of impatience while learning is that it takes a lot of time to learn and perfect a new piece. Learning a new piece and just moving on to another without perfecting it is a lot easier. Another reason that such people move quickly from piece to piece is that sheet music is not very helpful when the piece is more advanced. If they work on memorizing the piece as they learn it, they will find it much easier to play any new piece they come across. Their ability to perform will also improve, and they are more likely to have a successful future as a pianist. If you can develop the ability to memorize and learn music fast, you will be better able to perform and make music for the rest of your life. Memorizing can make a lot of difference between someone who is a professional and one who is still not proficient enough in their piano skills.

There is another general benefit that you should consider when it comes to memorizing. A lot of research has shown that the practice of memorizing helps in brain development for young people. For older people, it helps to reduce the pace of deterioration that comes with aging. To put it simply, memorizing will grant you a better memory while you are young and help ward away memory loss as you grow older. The more you practice memorizing, the more efficient your memory becomes, and this increases your intelligence quotient as well. Unlike what some people think, memorizing is not an ability that is restricted to some people. Every person can memorize and improve this skill. Many techniques help to improve your skills and how you can memorize them. As an aspiring pianist, you should try these out so it can help you memorize your music better. Once you are able to use memorization as a tool while playing the piano, you will start seeing your adeptness increase rapidly.

Video: Piano Finger Positions and More

To access the supporting video please visit the following link:

https://youtu.be/F4PS6LRUJ1Q

The correct way to position your fingers on the piano. Discover what the right distance and height is from the piano. In addition you will learn specific ways to move your arms, fingers and body. You will play exactly the way a professional piano player does. Watch and watch again. If you don't have a piano you can still practice these exercises using a table or piano mobile application and following the video. Enjoy.

If you have difficulty accessing the videos please email me at djswindali@gmail.com

Chapter Five: Finger Exercises For Learning The Piano

If you are just beginning to learn how to play the piano, you must be wondering what finger exercises have to do with it if all you're doing is playing a musical instrument. However, what you need to know is that playing the piano involves a lot of different finger movements. An aspiring pianist is akin to an athlete. Just as how an athlete must work out by running sprints or lifting weights, an aspiring pianist must exercise the muscles in his hand. It is only when they do this that they can become better at playing the piano.

There are many reasons why a piano player needs to perform finger exercises. For starters, it greatly diminishes the possibility of you hurting your fingers and picking up injuries while you are playing. Even the most popular pianists that you could think of constantly perform finger exercises to keep their technique sharp, and consistently doing these exercises if you are a beginner can also help you improve your playing technique rapidly.

There is more to playing the piano than just moving your fingers and playing the notes. The piano is a musical instrument that requires the utilization of the entire arm, the hands, the wrists, and your fingers. These parts must move synchronously together, so you can play the notes correctly. If you have aspirations of playing the piano for a long period or becoming a professional musician, you must regularly perform these finger exercises. You will notice the difference between a person playing the piano with poor technique and someone who has a proper technique and finger movements. The difference is that the former does not exercise regularly while the latter does. If you want to play professionally, you can never do it without having the correct finger techniques. Although all the different parts of the body that have been mentioned earlier are necessary for playing the piano effectively, it is the fingers and the finger muscles that are the primary muscles that do most of the work. The dexterity of these muscles can determine the extent of control we have over the sounds that we create while we are playing the piano.

Performing finger exercises can help you become better at playing the piano in more ways than one. Performing these finger exercises regularly can result in the overall improvement of finger coordination, strength, ability, and flexibility of your fingers. The improvement of these attributes can be reflected in your speed, sense of musicality, confidence levels, and the overall performance of the pianist. Essentially, finger exercises are one of the central aspects that you will need to be focusing on regularly, and it can help you significantly to become a good pianist in the same way that knowledge of musical notes, chords, scales, and arpeggios are.

In this chapter, we will be taking a detailed look at the different finger exercises from simple warm-up exercises that you can do regularly, or different finger/hand independence exercises that you can engage in, which are designed for improving specific techniques.

Proper Piano Finger Technique

Before we begin taking a look at the different finger technique exercises, we must develop a good understanding of what a good piano finger technique is exactly. The proper technique that is required for playing the piano efficiently is completely predicated on the basic principle that the fingers are always the main source of power while you are playing the piano. For beginners who have recently begun learning the basics and are self-taught pianists, such as you, several ideas will be laid down in the forthcoming sections that will seem completely new to you. Still, you will eventually become familiar and more adept at them with consistent practice.

On the other hand, people who have been playing the piano for a long time will find it hard to improve their technique if they adopt improper coaching. They may have had the wrong training or coach. However, with some time and practice, they eventually pick it up too.

The four basic elements of a proper piano finger technique are:

● Ensuring that your fingers are not resting in a flat or floppy position and that your knuckles are not straightened.

● Ensuring that all your fingers except the pinky are slightly angled at your knuckles. In some cases, you can straighten your pinky without affecting your technique.

● Always making sure that you are using your fingers as the primary driving source to press the keys of the piano, with the focus being on the muscle and not on your wrist, hand, or arm.

● Making sure that your elbows, shoulder, and forearms are placed in a relaxed position. Also, your fingers and your thumb should be prepared early before you eventually begin playing the piano.

Playing the piano involves extensive use of the fingers, and the small-scale muscles present on them as opposed to the other larger muscles that are present on the limbs. This is the most important concept that you should keep in the back of your mind as you progress through the journey of becoming an able pianist.

Common Mistakes That Occur in Piano Finger Techniques

People who have just begun taking piano lessons or who are self-learners are very prone to making many mistakes when it comes to piano finger techniques in the early stages. Most of them unknowingly end up developing and utilizing alternative techniques instead of traditional piano finger techniques. We have highlighted two of the most common and rampant of these techniques and advise you to be on the lookout so that you can stop yourself from adopting them and make corrections and adjustments if they do come up.

When people are just beginning to learn the piano, many students will tend to move their wrists towards an exceptionally high or low angle instead of changing the position of their hand. Regardless of the direction in which they move their wrists, some tension is created in the muscles due to a torsional effect. This effect comes with the wrist movements. This will ultimately lead to a decrease in speed and accuracy if you do not nip it at the bud.

Many beginners who have just started also tend to use their arms instead of playing with their fingers, which is the proper finger technique, as mentioned earlier. The use of arms tends to make the notes and sounds overly rhythmic. This overly rhythmic technique will produce different accents and unwanted beats, which normally shouldn't exist in the notes.

Warm-Up Exercises

Warm-up exercises are very good for relaxing the parts of the body, particularly the arms, wrists, and fingers, which we now know to be the most important drivers for playing the piano. These warm-up exercises are also used to help beginners to gradually ease into the necessary mindset that is required while practicing and playing the piano.

Speed Exercises

The speed exercises, as the name suggests, are those exercises that are aimed towards teaching you how to play fast passages of notes successfully. Playing fast passages of music will involve the exaggeration of the circular and rotational motion of the wrists that is normally required for playing passages at a slower tempo and the minimization of these same motions to achieve an increased speed.

To increase the speed at which you can play, you will have to be very familiar with the proper hand motions involved in playing the piano. One thing that every student will learn in the journey of learning to play the piano is that most pianists draw lots of circles. While you are playing the piano, the right hand is in constant motion and drawing imaginary circles even while playing simple scales. When you are playing a note that ascends, the wrist of your hand will scoop down. When the same notes are being played in the opposite direction, the wrist will attain an upward motion instead of scooping downward. The left hand, however, will be moving rotationally so that the wrist is rocked in a backward and forward movement. To be able to play faster while still maintaining proper techniques, it is necessary to make as few exaggerated motions as possible, and also to propel forwards faster than you usually do.

Finger/Hand Independence Exercises

The finger/hand independence exercises are those exercises that are done to strengthen the different muscles of your finger.

Piano Finger Exercises

The following exercises are the most popular piano finger exercises that you can try if you are very new to playing the piano. You should always endeavor to perform these different exercises at a consistent and comfortable tempo instead of trying to go fast straight away.

5 Note Pentascales with One Finger for Each Note

This particular exercise involves the student using only one finger to play the piano while also keeping a close ear on the output of what is being played.

You should try to vary your dynamic ranges using only your finger muscles as opposed to using the entirety of your shoulder and arms to achieve the variations. While this exercise may seem to be very easy and straightforward, people having inherently weak hand muscles will find it quite challenging to perform these exercises in the initial stages.

Ascending and Descending Pentascales

Once you improve how you move your fingers using the exercise above, the next thing you must do is practice playing the ascending and descending pentacles using your lowest finger. Remember to continue your movements by using the finger next to the lowest until the highest finger. You should do this using the fingers of both hands in order to develop in both of them.

A pianist requires all ten fingers and both hands to play the piano. If you favor the fingers of any particular hand, it will work as a disadvantage and only require more work to bring the other hand up to the mark. This means you should use your left-hand pinky as well as your Right-Hand Thumb together. You must ensure that you use all your fingers and both your thumbs. You have to work on using all the proper fingering techniques than have been taught in this book. Play the scales in opposite directions using both hands as this is good practice.

You Should Play Every Third Note and Skip Every Other Note

This is a finger exercise that you should keep practicing until you become adept at it. Once you are familiar with this exercise, try playing a pentascale in thirds. It is quite simple since you only have to play every other note while skipping every other note. This exercise will allow you to discipline your fingers so you can play every legato-connected note. While this exercise may seem very straightforward and simple, you should not be deceived by it since it is not as easy as it looks. This exercise may take your time to master, but it will be worth it. Take your time and keep practicing until you get the hang of it. Don't give up just because it takes a little more time than expected.

Utilize a Form of Finger Position as You Play the Piano

This is the next finger exercise that you have to try. First, place all your fingers at a level playing position. Don't put your fingers on the keys, but just keep them at the level of playing position. Your fingers should be in the proper piano playing position so that the knuckles closest to the fingertips after bent the way they would be while playing. Maintain the finger position and raise your entire hand before letting it fall on to the keyboard. Repeat the procedure at a lower height if your position gets disrupted, or your knuckles come apart.

This exercise will help you learn to play the piano by holding a firm finger position. Once you master this exercise, it will help improve your ability to play without any tension or extra arm weight. As you drop your fingers on the keys, it helps you focus completely on achieving a solid finger position.

Over-Legato

So you will be learning to play every note sequentially while making sure that one overlaps to the other. For example, consider the C major pentascale. While playing this, your thumb will depress a certain key as you hold that key until you play the index finger. After that, you release the thumb while keeping the index finger in the same position and then start playing with your middle finger. Then you play with the one after it. You should continue to use all the fingers in your hand. This over legato exercise is very helpful in learning and becoming more aware of your fingers. Once you develop more awareness, you'll also be better able to control every finger on your hand on an individual basis. You will learn how to use every finger individually so that it does not get in the way of your playing. This exercise is not easy and will require some effort and patience before you can master it. You might not get it immediately, but with assistant practice, you will eventually get better.

Full Scales

Practice this exercise to increase the speed and accuracy that you play with. You will have to practice the full scales simultaneously while preparing your thumb to play. The C major scale will be used as an example in this exercise. D is the first note on the scale, so play this first note using your index finger on the right hand and then brace your thumb finger as you get ready to play the F note next. Every scale should be rehearsed similarly until you get comfortable enough to play this way without thinking about it. As we said before, it will improve your speed and accuracy for playing the piano. If you want to be better at playing the piano and also play faster, then you must master this exercise.

Play 2 Notes at the Same Time Using the Same Hand

As you learn to be an efficient pianist, you will have to learn to play two notes simultaneously at some point or another. This is why you must practice and learn how to do this using the same hand while ensuring that the other fingers do not interfere while you play and are relaxed. Fingers do not usually work independently when there is more than one involved. This is why you have to keep practicing this piano finger exercise so you can master using those fingers independently of the others. The pinky finger is one that you will have to struggle with a little more than the others. This is because this finger is more stubborn and tends to interfere with what you do. This is why you will have to pay close attention to the pinky finger and control it while conducting the exercise.

Video: Finger Exercises

To access the supporting video please visit the following link:

https://youtu.be/eaxn3tTN_JY

In this supporting video Sorn Buranadham shows you how you can better at playing the piano through performing finger exercises. discover the four basic elements of correct piano finger technique. you will also find seven more supporting exercises that you can try right away. These all directly relate to the previous chapter. If you don't have a piano you can still practice these exercises using a table or piano mobile application and following the video. Enjoy.

If you have difficulty accessing the videos please email me at djswindali@gmail.com

Chapter Six: Chords

Piano Chords

Chords are one of the most important parts of any music. They come in all varieties and genres of music played or created with instruments. The melody line is played with several chord progressions whenever a song is played using any instrument. The basic needs to fulfill when you write music are the melody and chords.

The dealing out of a song is at least with two instruments. Regardless of how basic they are, one is to produce the melody, and another one is for the chord. Though the octave at which these two works vary from each other, including a piano and a keyboard, these two ingredients will be processed better via the same instruments if the musician or the player knows in-depth about these ingredients. Without a sense of these, it will not be possible to process both these ingredients to put them together on an instrument. Melody could also be generated using a voice; that is singing a song.

The chord will enable a musician to play the same melody on another instrument. It also makes it easier for a vocalist to sing the melody. A chord is always played along with the melody. However, while this is usual, but this is not what happens always.

Whenever we are talking about chords, it means that we are talking about one or more notes being played together at the same moment in that particular instrument. For example, we are talking about the piano. When the keys of a piano are pressed, the hammers or the striking pins connected to it strike the strings of the piano, and that eventually results in sound generation. So regarding the piano, whenever a pianist presses down two or more keys at a time on the instrument, he will have played a chord.

Chords are a group of notes that you play in a synchronized way so that you produce a harmony. But the harmony is generated only when these notes complement each other; chords give melody to the music and as well rhythm to a song. Two note chords are referred to as dyads, for example, power chords. Triads are quite basic and can include both major and minor chords. Also, there are four-note chords that go the major seven or minor seven chords.

The most commonly played chords on the piano are the Triads. It means three different notes, unlike each other, are played together, and each of these notes is distinct and quite different from one another. There are only one root note and the other two chords which fall at intervals of a third and a fifth away and above of that root note. It should always be kept in mind that the chords have to be in synchronization and balance one another to produce a pleasing sound.

Chord Knowledge

When we say chord knowledge, it means the knowledge of which particular note structures which chords, the development in which these chords produce sound, as well the names of the chords. There are a lot of chords to mention, and it would not be practical to talk about each and every one of them in this book, though the table below gives you a basic idea about what chord knowledge is. And this will, hopefully, get you started on your drive toward developing the chord knowledge.

Name	Formula	Examples of Notes (in Key C)	Emotion evoked
Major	I – III – V	C – E – G	Happy, gaiety, fullness
Minor	I – bIII – V	C – Eb – G	Sadness, resolve
Major 7	I – III – V – VII	C – E – G – B	Melancholy, smoothness

Different Types of Chords

There are different kinds of chords and several ways of classifying them. Some chords are dissonant, and so are not exactly pleasant to listen to, and those who are harmonious, which means that they are pleasing to the ears. There are also two-note chords, three-note chords, and so on. There are even broken chords. Below, we will examine some of the different types of chords.

Two-Note Chords

Another name of these type of chords is intervals. For those people who are fluent with the knowledge of music, a range is a gap, which is there between two pitches. Depending on how many there are and the quality of those, the naming of these intervals is done. For example, an interval is referred to as a major third. It has a major quality and the number three that represents that there are three notes that a particular interval has. To calculate this, you must consider the calculation lines of the musical staff and their positions of the note that make up for that particular interval.

For example, imagine you are playing note C and G, The number of the interval of this note is a "fifth," C, D, E, F, and G there are five notes lie in between these two notes. These notes fundamentally have five staff positions successively along with that of the notes that were played – C and G. And, the number will be having any of the following terms: perfect, augmented, diminished, major, and minor. As mentioned earlier, the name of an interval depends on both the number and quality.

Chords That Have More Than Three Notes

Tertian or tetrads chords can have notes of three. These names include altered tone clusters, tone chords, added tone chords, extended chords, and even seventh chords.

Major Chords

Of all the chords, the most commonly played chords in the world today are either the major ones or minor. Major chords will be comprised of the three notes, a root note, a third note, and a fifth note. Also, note that chords are also named like that. The root takes the middle part, that is the center stage. So, for example, a chord that is named as 'C major' has a C root, and this root chord will also be the lowest note it has. The next one is the third tone. This third tone will be either of the C major scale or an E.

And the last composition is of a major chord is the fifth tone. That'll either be the fifth tone of C major scale or G tone. No matter what the root note is, major chords will always have a major sound. And this is because half steps present from one note to the other will always remain the same, from the root node to the third this half step is four, While it is three When it is from 3rd to the 5th note. The gap between the root and the third is called a major third. The gap between the third and fifth is called the minor 3rd. It is the same for all the 12 tones on the chromatic scale of a piano.

It will also have a fifth, which will be either the fifth tone of the C major scale or a G tone. Major chords will always have a major sound, no matter the note that forms the root. The reason for this is that the number of half steps that will be present from one note to the other will remain the same no matter what. This half step is four between the root note and the third while it is three when going from the third to the fifth. The interval between the root and third is known as a major 3rd. The interval that exists between the third and fifth is known as the A minor third. This goes for all twelve tones that make up the chromatic scale of the piano.

To explain, imagine playing D major chord, by now we already know that the root tone is D, from here counting four steps to get the third, which is F sharp, and three half steps from F sharp is at A tone.

Another example, a black key this time, let's imagine we are playing E-flat Key. The root will be E tone, four half steps from it will get you to G tone, which is the third tone, while three half steps from there will be the B- flat tone

Minor Chords

Minor chords are like the reverse of major chords like the inverse, to play a minor chord again we have to start from the root and go three steps to the minor third, and again four half steps to the minor fifth. For example, to play a C minor chord, we will have to start from C as the root, of course, then three steps from C that will be E-flat tone, for the major third; four half steps from this is the G tone.

To put it briefly, play the minor chords, decreasing the middle tone by one-half step, which will result in playing a minor chord by the piano.

Diminished Chords

Certain genres and types of music like jazz use these. To play a diminished chord, you will have to use two minor thirds. For example, to play a C diminished, play the C tone, which is the root tone, then the E-flat tone, and then the G-flat tone.

Augmented Chords

Using two major thirds results in augmented chords. Which are in the opposite direction to the diminished chords.

Dissonant Chords

Dissonant chords are those whose quality varies from the sound produced. That is chords sound, which is not particularly harmonious. As such, qualities are mentioned as either diminished or augmented. This sound is odd and unpleasant. Still, they do have their use in music. Some musicians make use of these chords at planned positions in music to make the music more attractive and enticing.

Broken Chords

As the name suggests, this type of chord is with notes that are not played simultaneously. This means that the chord is broken into many pieces in a sequence called "arpeggio." This term means that you split the chords in the melody in rising order. Though arpeggios are broken chords. The reverse is not the same, as broken chords are much more than just arpeggios.

Chord Progressions

The organization of chords is called as chord progressions. This means that a series of ordered chords is referred to as a harmonic progression. The reason for this is that chord progressions are vital for the generation of harmony in classical and American music.

Video: Chords

To access the supporting video please visit the following link:

https://youtu.be/80bHdEYx_Uc

In this supporting video Sorn Buranadham shows you the chords you need to play piano and how you can use them. Discover the main chords most commonly used by piano players. These all directly relate to the previous chapter. If you don't have a piano you can still practice these exercises using a table or piano mobile application and following the video. Enjoy.

If you have difficulty accessing the videos please email me at djswindali@gmail.com

Chapter Seven: Rhythm

Most people are familiar with the concept of beats without being aware of it. Think of when you hear some music and start moving to it. What you are dancing to is the beat or rhythm of the music. Rhythm is something that we all seem to have an innate ability to connect with and feel. However, when it comes to the piano, you have to have a deeper understanding of the beat. Beats are regular intervals of sounds or rhythm. The most important aspect to grasp is that they are regular. Every piece of music will have its beat, and the beat may go faster or slower, but you will still know that it exists. However, you have to be familiar with tempo to know the beat. The tempo will tell you how fast you should play and help you count how many beats are there in every measure. If there is a measure with four-quarter notes, you have to play the notes in a steady rhythmic pattern. However, you can play at a fast or slow tempo without changing the steadiness of its rhythm. You must look at the time signature after this. You will know the number of beats in each measure, and will also know the type of note that will get the beat. The time signature will be present at the beginning of your music before the first measure and beside the clef signs for the hands.

Rhythm is a combination of everything mentioned above. It creates a pattern that is recognizable when you organize the notes in a particular piece. Notes do not make sense without rhythm because there would be no structure to fit into.

Video: Rhythm

To access the supporting video please visit the following link:

https://youtu.be/e_CjOllXSXM

In this supporting video Sorn Buranadham shows you how to identify the tempo and follow the beat of a song. Discover some of the most common time signatures including 4/4, beats, bars and much more important aspects of playing in time. In addition you will learn about the way songs are constructed and how you can easily follow along with them to make sure you are playing in time. This relates to the previous chapter. Watch and watch again. If you don't have a piano you can still practice these exercises using a table or piano mobile application and following the video. Enjoy.

If you have difficulty accessing the videos please email me at djswindali@gmail.com

Chapter Eight: Patterns

Learning more left-hand accompaniment patterns is important when you want to play the piano.

Fixed and Broken Chords

Chords are the easiest left-hand accompaniment regardless of whether you play them as arpeggios or straight chords. You can start with basic chords and then discover what inversions work better for you without having to move your left hand all over the keyboard. Also, try experimenting with different rhythmic patterns. The texture can be changed, and you can add some variety in the left hand. Use the octave, fifth, and root notes of the chord scale for every chord symbol. Now, form an up and down pattern throughout the piece that you are playing. This pattern can be played for fast as well as slow music.

Chord Picking

When it comes to country music, left-hand chord picking is well suited. However, this pattern can be applied to any other music as well. A lot of chords include a root note with third and fifth intervals. These three elements have to be known if you want to try chord picking successfully. To play this pattern, you have to break a chord into the root note with two top notes. On beat 1, you should play the root note, and on beat 2, you should play the two top notes. You can try something different while playing on beat three so that it sounds more impressive. Try using this pattern on some piece of music to try it out. You will see the bouncy rhythm it creates without you having to keep looking at your hands.

Octave Hammering

It is a fun and straightforward groove if you are only playing chords with your right hand. However, this pattern is not practical if you are playing something more complicated, like a melody with your right hand. For octave hammering, you have to place your left hand in an octave position. Your thumb and pinky finger should be ready on the two notes, and your wrist should be loose enough for it to bounce with the right rhythm. Your hand should remain in the octave position when the chord changes, and you are moving to the next octave set. You can try anything from half notes to whole notes or eight notes while playing the octaves and see what sounds best to you. When you become familiar with harmony, you can add some left-hand octave patterns with octaves on the notes of the chords.

Bouncy Patterns

You can also try a rock type of sound pattern. This uses the fifth, octave, and sixth intervals of the chord, you can create a good bass pattern.

Melodic Bass

Some widely used patterns are even more famous than the leads that they accompany. You just need 3 notes from every chord scale, and these are the root, fifth, and sixth. These can be played back and forth repeatedly.

Chapter Nine: Scales

Musical Scales

The term scale was derived from the Latin word scala for ladder or stairs. It is for this reason why staves denote scales. You can also think of these similar to climbing a ladder. To put it simply, musical scales are a collection of notes that are ordered according to fundamental frequency or pitch. A musical scale is the tonal basis of music and melodies and harmonies can be developed from it. You need to learn how to identify musical scales so that you can orient yourself amongst the notes. This provides a foundation for compromise and improvisation. You do not have to be able to read notes before reading musical scales, but it is more important to get acquainted with scales before reading notes. You should also note that it is not necessary to learn many chords, but knowing some basic chords will help you memorize musical scales much easier. This is because chords are derived from musical scales.

Usually, a scale will be made up of seven notes that are called the major and minor notes. A scale is octave repeating, which means that the pattern of notes will remain the same regardless of the position of the keys on the keyboard. A full-scale piano usually has 88 keys in total, but there are only twelve notes. These twelve notes will be repeated from bass to treble and from low tones to high tones. While playing the piano, you will usually be using the enharmonic notes. Two sharps or two flats will often be used in adjunction to notes that are already described in a piano score. These are called double flats or double sharps. For instance, if you consider the D sharp note, the key will include the D sharp note as well as the D note. However, if you want to make functional in scores, it will be D#

and C##. Otherwise, you will play D# instead of a D note. Before identifying specific scales, you have to learn the unique sequence of intervals.

Terms to Note

Key

Key is the note on which a scale is built. Usually, a key is the first note in any scale.

Tonic

Tonic refers to the first or lowest note on any specific scale.

Mode

A mode is an alternate way in which a scale can be used well, and it also includes adding some type of melody to the scale.

Enharmonic Equivalents

Enharmonic equivalents are just another way of saying similar notes. For instance, the C sharp note is similar to the D flat note.

Scale Degrees

Scale degrees are the special name given to each note in the scale. Roman numerals are used for giving this special name to the notes.

Tonic (I)

It is the first note in the scale, and the scale is built upon it. It is also called the root.

Supertonic (II)

It is above the root and is the second scale degree.

Median (III)

It is found in between the dominant and tonic and is the third scale degree.

Subdominant (IV)

It is found next to the dominant and is fifth under the tonic. It is the fourth scale degree.

Dominant (V)

It is the fifth scale degree.

Submedian (VI)

It is also called the super median and is the sixth scale degree.

Subtonic (VII)

It is the seventh scale degree that leads back to the tonic and is also called the leading tone at times.

Natural Scales

The two major types of scales are the major and minor scales. The difference between these two scales is in the third, sixth, and seventh degrees. Major scales use major interval degrees while minor scales use minor interval degrees. Since these are the most basic parts of music study, they are called natural scales. The natural major scale is also called the diatonic major scale. The natural minor scale is also called the diatonic minor scale. Diatonic means moving in the tonic. So when you use the word diatonic, it suggests that that note is part of a natural major scale or a natural minor scale. Diatonic scales make use of seven pitches, including two half steps and five whole steps.

Examples of Musical Scales

C Major

The C note is the tonic or key in this scale. The scale is Major, and it forms the C Major Scale. The scale and key end up as heptatonic scales if they exist without anything else.

Pentatonic F# Minor

The F sharp is the key or tonic here, and the pentatonic minor is utilized here. The pentatonic minor is a variation of the minor scale. Since the scale is minor, it is similar to the heptatonic or natural minor except for the two pitches in the scale.

Different Types of Scales

Musical scales exist in many different types. Here you will learn about the major types of scales that are important for any pianist.

Pentatonic

The pentatonic musical scale is used quite commonly in oriental or folk music. It uses five notes or pitches. In the pentatonic scale, two notes are removed from the heptatonic musical scale, and only five notes remain. The notes that are removed will vary for the minor and major scales. In the pentatonic major scales, the fourth and seventh notes are removed from the heptatonic scale. In the pentatonic minor scale, the second and sixth notes are removed from the heptatonic minor scales.

Hexatonic

The hexatonic musical scale is commonly used in western music and consists of six notes or pitches.

Heptatonic

The heptatonic musical scale is usually used in modern-day western music and has seven notes or pitches. This scale is also called a natural scale. It includes the natural F# major and natural c major. Both beginners and professionals can use this scale quite well. For heptatonic minor scales, the key signature is W-H-W-W-H-W-W. For heptatonic major scales, the key signature is W-W-H-W-W-W-H.

Octatonic

The octatonic musical scale is common in jazz or modern classical music. It has eight notes or pitches.

Modes

Modes are sets of melodic characteristics applied to musical scales. However, the concept of modes is quite intricate and complex. The following are some important points on modes:

W stands for the whole step while H stands for half steps.

Ionian

Ionian mode is the natural major scale. The interval sequence here is W-W-H-W-W-W-H.

Dorian

Dorian mode has a different sixth pitch but is the natural minor scale. It has the interval sequence W-H-W-W-W-H-W.

Phrygian

The Phrygian mode is the natural minor scale but with a different second pitch. The interval sequence for this mode is H-W-W-W-H-W-W.

Mixolydian

Mixolydian mode is the natural major scale, with the seventh pitch being different. The interval sequence for it is W-W-H-W-W-H-W.

Lydian

Lydian mode is the natural major scale, but the fourth pitch is different. The interval sequence for it is W-W-W-H-W-W-H.

Locrian

The Locrian mode is the mode without the fifth pitch. The interval sequence for it is H-W-W-H-W-W-W.

Aeolian

The Aeolian mode is the natural minor scale with the interval sequence W-H-W-W-H-W-W.

Video: Musical Scales

To access the supporting video please visit the following link:

https://youtu.be/ITLbkpFP8Y4

In this supporting video Sorn Buranadham explains and shows you some examples of Musical Scales. You will see exactly the notes for each of those scales on the piano. Discover the C Major, Pentatonic F# Minor and various other different types of scales. If you don't have a piano you can still practice these exercises using a table or piano mobile application and following the video. Enjoy.

If you have difficulty accessing the videos please email me at djswindali@gmail.com

Chapter Ten: Tone, Rhythm and Staccato

Tone

One important feature in musical sounds is tone. The tone is considered the discerning factor. It is used to determine the appropriateness of the music based on the properties of the sound. Some say that the players of instruments like the piano cannot influence the tone of any musical note that they play. However, it is an accepted fact that two different musicians playing the same instrument will never play the same tone even if they are playing the same musical piece. The difference in their tone is caused by other factors that are outside of the player's control.

Some of these varying factors include the make of the instrument, the tuning of the instrument, and the notes being played. It is not important to argue about if the pianist can change or influence the tone of the note they are playing. What is important is determining if they are playing a single note or a group of notes. More often than not, when we are listening to different tones, it is a different group of notes. When you understand this, it helps you get a better grasp of what a tone is. This allows you to understand that a tone is produced when a player influences creative musical notes. Musicians usually find that the tones they produce will generally rely on the content of the notes they play along with accuracy and control. It concludes that a tone is the function of musical notes as well as the player's level of perception.

When tones are simplified to musical notes, you will see that every note can be influenced in several different ways, and this, in turn, affects the tone. The notes can be changed by altering the harmonic content. This means that the note changes when you play louder or softer. Using damper pedals is another method of doing this. Once you get familiar with musical notes and music, you will see that all the methods mentioned here will affect the timbre of the note. Also, remember that timbre is a functional component of tones. The tuner can modify the timbre in two ways. One way is where they alter the tune, and the other way is where the density of the hammer covering felts is changed to produce brighter tones. If the tuning is altered, it also influences the stretch or the amount of detuning among unisons. A larger stretch will produce brighter sounds. When a piano gives out ugly sounds, it usually means that there is an inadequate stretch.

You also have to consider if the tone of a note can be changed with the effect of downstrokes. The downstroke is one of the major components of keystrokes and is a basic movement that creates sound while playing the piano. The downstroke will produce the actual sound from the piano because it controls how the hammer hits the string. Since the hammer of the piano is considered to be in free flight, many people believe that the hammer has a strong influence on the tone control. Some believe that tones are uncontrollable. They argue that the production of a musical note is affected by the speed of a free moving hammer. However, no one was able to prove the theory of the free moving hammer. A major factor that affects the tone is the bend of a hammer shank. For producing a loud note, the shank probably bends when the hammer goes into free motion, and this causes an effective increase in the mass of the hammer as it strikes on a string. The movement of the hammer gains more power from positive bending movements, and this pushes the hammer forward while the flex recovers once the hammer jack is released. The difference between the tone of a note played in staccato, and that played deep is quite noticeable because the hammer bend is already negative by the time the hammer hits the string.

Rhythm

Now let's talk about rhythm. The word rhythm was derived from the rhythms, which is a Greek word that means "to flow." rhythm can be defined as a regularly repeating pattern of sound. There are many books as well as musical manuals that have created the notion that rhythm is some sort of function of talent in a person or something that they can achieve only if they train or practice endlessly. However, rhythm is, in fact, an art that involves the practice of reading music precisely along with accurate counting concerning time. There is a lot of hard work and sophistication that goes into the creation of rhythmic sounds, and it should not be underestimated. However, you should not be intimidated when it comes to rhythm regardless of whether you are a beginner or someone with experience. If you just put in some effort, you can learn more about rhythm. Indeed, the art of rhythm is not very simple, and there are many problems when some music score lacks indications for rhythm, as the reader would expect. This is why it has been inferred that most problems related to rhythm arise from the lack of information on its musical scores, and this makes them harder to read. When the rhythm is not represented properly, the brain is occupied with more conspicuous thoughts, and there is very little space for it to think clearly about them. This is especially so when the music score has technicalities that the player is not familiar with. However, the unfortunate aspect of this kind of problem is that you cannot change the mistake. It also flows into any other music because of habit. Rhythm is majorly used in music to produce different music using variation and manipulation.

Rhythm has two major components that you need to remember - time and accents. These components are used in formal and logical forms in music. The logical form is an important element that is harder to explain. The formal part is much simpler but just as important as the logical form. Many aspiring pianists forget to give the required amount of attention to this, and thus their music ends up disconcerting.

Formal Timing

The formal timing of rhythm is determined by the time signature that is indicated at the beginning of the score. The time signature is used for indicating the number of beats in a bar and the notes that represent a beat. Important time signatures to remember are the waltz, cut time, and common time.

Formal Accents

Every time signature will have its formal accent. For instance, think of a convention where one is the loudest, and this is followed by 2, 3, and so on. Here, the Viennese waltz will have 133 as the formal accent, and the accent is placed on the first beat.

Logical Timing and Accents

This is the change in loudness and timing from formal rhythm. The rhythm produced will have a vivid change in structure in the composer's work. It is commonly seen in music and is often used by musicians even though it is not necessary. Accelerate and decelerate are some popular examples that exhibit logical rhythmic timing. Accelerate signifies the increase in the excitement of things while decelerate signifies the tail end of a music score or rubato.

Legato

The term legato refers to a smooth, flowing manner where there are no breaks between notes. It is a kind of melodic exhibition strategy. Every note is played to the maximum length and then mixes into whatever it pursues. This explains how melodic notes can be played together and sung easily together. It means that there is no interceding quiet as a player moves from one note to another. For slurred execution, the legato procedure is required. It does not forbid the repetition of a single note, though. If succeeding notes are connected, this technique can be achieved. Until the second note is played, the first note should not be lifted. This is an important principle to remember. Many great musicians have had an opinion on this particular technique. Fraser advocated a considerable overlap of two notes. Legato is a habit and has to be developed into your skill. Test different notes and overlaps to see what produces the best sounds. Constant practice will help to develop this into a habit that will easily be carried out at will. The basic keystroke is very important for legato.

Staccato

The opposite of legato is staccato. Here one note does not stream into the other. Every note is individually sounded out, and a little rest is deliberately left near the end of its dispensed term. Compared to legato playing, staccato playing is much more sprightly and percussive. Staccato is also fit to other older styles of music like gavottes, mazurkas, and Viennese dances. In more mainstream music, it includes nation, twang, hip-hop, and funk.

In staccato, a short musical sound is delivered with no continuity by skipping the finger off the key. A lot of piano books talk about staccato, but very few manage to explain it properly. The ordinary and hard are the two documentations for staccato. The jack is not discharged in either of these. The finger tends to go down and up a lot more quickly in hard staccato. In ordinary staccato, unlike in hard staccato, the key drop is mostly down. The damper also comes back more quickly to the strings, and it brings a shorter length of the note. The mallet bobs around because the backcheck is not locked in, and this makes redundancies more precarious at certain velocities. If you happen to find it difficult while dealing with rehashed staccatos, don't push yourself too fast. It could be because of some inappropriate recurrence where the mallet ricochets in the wrong way. If you change the speed, the measure of the key drop, and so forth, it might allow you to solve this issue. Usually, in typical staccato, the damper is restored onto the strings quite rapidly by the action of gravity. When it comes to hard staccato, the damper aims to return a lot more rapidly and is ricocheted off the top rail of the damper. The sled shank flex may be negative at string contact, and this makes the mallet mass lighter. Thus many types of tones can be created with staccato. Similarly, staccato changes everything from the movement of the mallet and jack to that of the damper and backcheck.

Depending on how the staccato is played; it is divided into three types:

● Finger staccato

● Wrist staccato

● Arm staccato

For the most part, the finger staccato will be played with the finger while keeping the arm still. In wrist staccato, there is more wrist activity. For arm staccato, the activity begins at the upper arm. While you move from the beginning to the end, more mass is included behind your fingers, and thus the finger method gives you the lightest and quick staccato. It is better for single and delicate notes. The arm method will give you a heavier inclination and is better for louder entries and harmonies that have several notes. However, it is the slowest. The wrist staccato is in the middle. Most piano players will join all of the three. The amplitude of the wrist and arm must be diminished correspondingly to play quick staccato since they are slower. Some instructors don't prefer using the wrist staccato and instead lean towards using the arm staccato more. However, it is a much better choice to use a blend of all the staccatos. For example, you can diminish weakness if you change from one staccato to another, even though changing fingers is the usual strategy for reducing weariness. When you rehearse staccato, first practice the three staccatos then choose which one you want to use. Otherwise, find the best way to consolidate the three staccatos. Since arm weight cannot be used for staccato, your unfaltering body is the best reference. This is how the body plays a big role in playing staccatos.

Arpeggios are a type of broken chord where the notes composing the chord are played in an ascending or descending order. The span of an arpeggio can be more than an octave. Arpeggios are groups of notes that are played consecutively in an up or down pitch. Being able to play arpeggios in the right way can be a little complex technically. This is why arpeggios are suitable for learning hand motions like pull, thrust, and cartwheel.

Chromatic scales are a twelve-tone scale or a musical scale that has twelve pitches with each semitone lying below or above its adjacent pitch. The notes in an equal-tempered chromatic scale will be spaced equally.

Video: Tone, Legato, Arpeggio, Staccato

To access the supporting video please visit the following link:

https://youtu.be/5SPDnc44OhU

In this supporting video Sorn Buranadham explains Tone, Legato, Arpeggio and Staccato. Discover how notes can be changed by altering the harmonic content with damper pedals, different playing methods, special techniques and much more. See how it's done in the video. If you don't have a piano you can still practice these exercises using a table or piano mobile application and following the video. Enjoy.

If you have difficulty accessing the videos please email me at djswindali@gmail.com

Chapter Eleven: Practice

Piano Chords and Melodies

In music, chords and melodies are very important elements. Songs that are played on many different instruments usually have a melody line played over a chord progression series. Usually, chords and melodies are processed together in a song, and one instrument usually plays the chord while the melody is played on the other. On a piano, both these elements can be processed at the same time. The pianist needs to have accurate knowledge of melodies and chords for this. If they don't have enough knowledge, they will find it difficult to work on chords and melodies together.

Sound pitches are formed by combining chords, and this includes at least three different pitches. A chord progression is based on a series of chords. The piano has white and black keys that make up a half step or complete keys. A chord begins with a note and is a combination of different notes, including complete and half steps. Basic chords include three notes that are termed as a triad on the piano. Chords are usually based around the notes, and the start note is the root note.

A melody is a line of pitch that can be played with single or more instruments. A melody is usually high in sound pitch. Just like chords, the melody is essential to make the music sound complete. Pianists usually play the chords with their left hand while the melody is played with their right hand. By manipulating keys and notes, many types of melodies can be played on the piano.

Chord tones are usually designed with the same chord progressions. You have to identify the chord tones that sound good within the chord progression if you want to process any melody. Chords and melody are interlinked, and it is a better idea to base melodies on piano chords. Apart from chord-based melodies, pianists can also design melodies that have step movements and not chord tones. Such melodies would form the base for a fluid transition and would be separate from the chords played. One key difference between a melody and chord progression is that the former is based on a single line while the latter includes many lines of pitches.

A pianist needs to have a thorough knowledge of piano theory to experiment with melodies and chords on a piano. Some chords conflict with melody, and you can choose accordingly through trial and error.

How to Memorize

As we mentioned before, memorizing is an important tool for mastering the art of piano playing. Here are some tips to help you memorize piano music:

● From the first day that you start practicing playing the piano, have the intent of memorizing and internalizing the music. Don't wait until you finish learning the whole piece and then memorize it. It will give you a head start and help you remember it better if you begin from day one.

● Use the right fingering consistently. It is important to learn the piece while using the right fingering, or it will take you a lot longer to learn it. Instead of using different fingering every time you play it, write down the fingering on the score and use it consistently.

● Memorize all the articulations, dynamics, and any other markings on the page. Don't wait to master everything else until you have mastered the notes. Learn it all at the same time, even if it might seem a little tedious to do so. It will be tougher to go back and try to fix things later.

● Try playing the piece without the sheets in front of you. Don't rely on the music sheets all the time. Try keeping it aside at times and see how far you go without seeing it. Doing this repeatedly will help you memorize it better.

● Memorize small sections. Try memorizing four measures at a time. You can even memorize two at a time when you need to. As you keep doing this, you will be able to memorize the entire piece.

● Practice slowly. When you try to memorize while playing a fast tempo, it mostly strengthens your muscle memory, but this is not enough. It is harder to practice music slowly, and it allows you to strengthen your visual, intellectual, and tactile memory.

● Memorize hands separately. Quite often, the left hand is neglected, and this is the one you need to pay special attention to. Don't leave it to chance that the left hand will just follow the right hand automatically.

● Analyze music. You should analyze the music in different ways. Analyze the form first and then label the sections in the score, so it allows you to form a mental map in your head. Also, do a harmonic analysis using roman numerals.

How to Play a Song by Ear

Playing by ear is a desirable skill for musicians. You don't need to be born with the ability to do this. Playing by ear requires you to acquire certain skills, and these can all be learned over time. You will notice that some people seem to have the innate ability to play anything by ear when they hear it, but most others find this very difficult. While some are gifted with this talent, nothing beats hard work. The best thing you can do is repeatedly listen to music. If you are dedicated to ear training, it will help speed up the process.

The following are some skills that will help you:

● You will be able to hear the key of the music if you have strong absolute pitch

● You can pinpoint any notes in riffs or melodies if you have interval skills

● It is much easier to identify progressions with chord ear training

● Rhythm ear training will allow you to make out any strange phrasing or syncopation.

How to Play by Reading

Once you learn how to read sheet music, it unlocks a whole new world for you. It takes some time to become proficient at reading sheet music on sight but is a valuable skill to acquire for any musician. Learning the piano goes hand in hand with reading sheet music. If you want to tackle any piece of music, you have to memorize the notes. Learning to read sheet music is the first thing that you need to do to improve your piano skills.

The following steps will help you read sheet music and play the piano:

● Any white spaces should be labeled with FACE and EGBDF for treble clef. The treble clef shows you the notes to be played with your right hand. You need to get familiar with the letter names of all the spaces and lines when you begin. Label white spaces with FACE from the first space near the bottom of the page. Then going up, label the lines from the bottom line to the top line as EGBDF.

● Write down the note letter names. Write the letter names under the music notes of the right hand in treble clef. This is just for when you start out and not something you want to do in the long run.

● Memorize all the letter names and then move to bass clef. Once you memorize all the letter names for your right hand, start reading piano notes on the bass clef for your left hand.

● Name the spaces ACEGB and GBDFA. Name the spaces ACEGB at the bottom of the page. Name the lines from the bottom GBDFA.

● Label each finger in a hand diagram with 1-5. Label each finger on your right hand and left hand like 1-5. Right the numbers next to the letter names.

Advanced Songs

Once you start playing the piano, you will probably want to play some of your favorite music pieces. However, it may be tough to play more advanced pieces of music. If you master the basics, this will not be a big problem over time. The following are some tips to help you play advanced music:

● Allow yourself to be motivated by a piece of music that you love and want to learn. This motivation will feed your effort. Then make sure you brush up on your fundamentals and then try playing. Pick your song and start practicing. Don't choose something easy, but it should not be so hard that you give up too soon. Listen to the song repeatedly and also watch videos on how other pianists played it.

● Break it down. After choosing the music, start slicing it up. The brain tends to work at full throttle when you are playing the piano since you have to memorize new things constantly. If you break up the new piece into sections of 5-10 seconds, it is much easier to focus on and learn. Don't try to learn the whole thing at once. Once you finish a few sections, play them together. Keep doing this till you can play the whole piece.

● Make sure you can play separately with each hand. This is important before you start playing with both hands. When you try to learn a new complex piece with both hands, it can be too much for your brain to handle.

● Practice daily. If you practice regularly, you will get much better results. It will also help to maintain the flow of learning, and you will be able to learn the piece in a shorter time.

Video: How to Play a Song by Ear

To access the supporting video please visit the following link:

https://youtu.be/rU89_-IA3DI

In this supporting video Sorn Buranadham explains how to play a song by ear. There are some really great ways you can master this skill. Discover how to find out what key a song is in, the chords and then how to play it. In addition, learn how to play the melody, phrasing and much more. This video will show you how to train your ears like a professional. Watch and watch again. If you don't have a piano you can still practice these exercises using a table or piano mobile application and following the video. Enjoy.

If you have difficulty accessing the videos please email me at djswindali@gmail.com

Video: How to Play a Song by Reading

To access the supporting video please visit the following link:

https://youtu.be/ukSqbF-4lwl

In this supporting video Sorn Buranadham shows you how to play a song by reading. The key of C will be used to explain the basic concept of reading music theory. Discover how to read the treble clef, bass clef, divisions and some of the most common music terminology which will help you to read music. In the video you will find some really quick and easy ways to have you reading music in no time. This relates to the previous chapter. Watch and watch again. If you don't have a piano you can still practice these exercises using a table or piano mobile application and following the video. Enjoy.

If you have difficulty accessing the videos please email me at djswindali@gmail.com

Chapter Twelve: Piano Playing Strategies

If you want to become a good pianist as soon as possible, it is important to have a strategy. This means that you need a plan of action that is clearly defined. As you read on, you will learn of a strategy that was tried and tested by many other piano players. However, the more important thing to remember is that you can only become a good pianist if you practice constantly and judiciously. Just the intention of becoming a good player is not enough if you don't put in the work.

Define Your Goal

It is important to have a well-defined goal when you are beginning. Think of what level you want to achieve in a given amount of time. Consider the actual amount of time you are willing to put into practicing and where you want to go from that level. Think of these things before you even set out to learn the piano and be willing to dedicate as many hours as required to attain your goal.

Warm-Up

Warming up is the next part of your piano playing strategy. Don't play without warming up. It may be tempting just to start playing what you want, but this can cause carpal tunnel or tendinitis. When you warm up, it helps you prepare yourself to play further without endangering yourself.

Practice the Basics

Another essential aspect of the strategy is to practice the basics constantly. This includes scales, timing, and accuracy. Even master pianists make sure to practice piano basics so that it helps them get better. Always set aside time in the day to practice these basics and hone your skills.

Take it Slow

It is impractical to expect instant gratification. No one can learn the piano in a day. You have to take it slow and monitor your progress. You might get better at it at a slow pace, but there will be a definite improvement over time. If you want to master the art of playing the piano, don't rush through the process.

Learn from the Masters

For any aspiring pianist, it is important to listen to master pianists and learn from them. There will be certain pianists whose music you prefer over others. Listening and loving the music will help you stay inspired and learn a lot about the sounds created from a piano.

Take Breaks

Consistency and dedication are important, but piano playing should not become a chore. You should enjoy it without taking on too much at a time. Practice regularly but take breaks when you need to. The best thing you can achieve from music is happiness. Making it a chore will take the joy out of your music.

Chapter Thirteen: Tips and Common Mistakes

It takes a lot of work to learn the piano. There is a lot of room to learn, make mistakes, and grow in the beginning. Most beginners make a lot of mistakes while playing and practicing. We have put together some of the common mistakes that tend to occur and some tips on how you can avoid them.

Not Paying Attention to Correct Fingering

This is a common mistake that most beginners seem to repeat. They feel that it is unnecessary and uncomfortable, so they ignore the fingering. However, in the long run, it makes a lot of difference because it becomes much harder to play complex music pieces.

Assuming That the Clefs Refer to Hands

On a page of music, there will be two lines. One is for the right hand, and the other is for the left. For the most part, this is how to determine what you should play with each hand. However, clefs denote the octave that you will be playing and not the hand that you have to use.

Not Distinguishing Between Notes and Keys

You have to remember that notes are not the same things as keys. The keys are on the piano, and notes are on the page. Notes may take many different forms and are written in various ways.

Sticking to C Major

C major is probably the easiest key to play in songs since you don't have to bother with flats or sharps. However, all songs are not in C. you have to learn to play other keys properly as well.

Assuming Sharps and Flats are Black Keys

While this is usually the case, B sharp and F flat are white keys. So don't assume that every sharp and flat is a black key.

Neglecting Scales

Although scales can feel a little pointless or boring, they are essential in learning to play the piano. Anyone who wants to play the piano moderately well has to be proficient in the scales. Practicing the scales will help to improve dexterity and the ability to read and play.

Playing Everything Too Fast

Most people feel that being able to play the piano makes them an advanced player. However, this is not true. Not every musical piece is meant to be played fast. If you play a slow piece too fast, it does not sound pleasing to the audience who has to hear it. You should always count and use a metronome so that your tempo is right.

Playing with Flat Fingers

A lot of students start playing the piano with flat fingers. This means that their finger flatly extends from their hand, and this first knuckle is collapsed. If you play with flat fingers, it slows down your technique and can cause tension. You should always pay attention to this and play with curved fingers.

Sitting Too Close to the Piano

Pay attention to the distance at which you set from the piano. If you sit too close, you won't have enough space for your arms. It limits the range of motions and causes tension on your wrists as well.

Not Using Arm Weight

When you play the piano, you should be using the weight of your torso and arms. Fingers control the keys, but playing solely with finger strength will not produce the right kind of tone. You have to learn to channel your arm and bodyweight efficiently through the arms so that you can produce a large range of sounds and tones. It will also help to reduce the strain exerted on the fingers.

Keep all of the points mentioned above in mind so that you don't make these beginners' mistakes while playing the piano.

Video: Tips and Common Mistakes

To access the supporting video please visit the following link:

https://youtu.be/tW-3ydS2_WA

In this supporting video Sorn Buranadham reveals some of the most common mistakes and tips for piano players. Everyone needs to be aware of these things and be willing to put in the work. Discover how to warm up, exclusive tips that will help you to master the piano. In addition you will discover some of the most common mistakes and how you can avoid them. Keep all of this in mind so you can become the best you can. Watch and watch again. If you don't have a piano you can still practice these exercises using a table or piano mobile application and following the video. Enjoy.

If you have difficulty accessing the videos please email me at djswindali@gmail.com

Conclusion

Now that you have finished reading the book, you can get started with putting it all into practice. You have enough knowledge to give you a head start amongst most beginners. A lot of people underestimate the importance of learning more about the piano before they start playing it. This book was written to help you learn where the piano came from, how it works, and how you can get as skilled at playing it as possible. By now, you have a lot of knowledge about the most important aspects of the piano, like chords, tones, scales, rhythm, etc. You should also have a good idea about the strategies that will help you learn and play the piano better.

Make use of all the information in the book and video to hone your piano playing skills. It is a good guide for beginners and will also help other pianists who want to improve their skills. Once you acquire a piano for yourself, make sure to take care of it and utilize it by practicing regularly. Playing the piano is a gratifying activity that you will never tire of and something that will allow you to please everyone around you as well.

Remember that what you put in you get out. watch all the supporting videos and take the time to study this book. don't just read and watch one time. Keep re-reading and re-watching the supporting videos to really install the knowledge into your brain. As you practice and combine the learning you will naturally become better. Make sure you also stick to regularly practicing everyday at a certain time. I wish you all the best and look forward to hearing from you.

Resources

https://bestdigitalpianoguides.com/piano-chords-and-melodies/

https://takelessons.com/blog/reading-piano-notes

https://www.dictionary.com/browse/legato

https://www.flowkey.com/en/piano-tips

https://www.musical-u.com/learn/topic/how-to/play-by-ear/

https://www.voicesinc.org/piano-learning-mistakes/

https://www.liveabout.com/chord-definition-2701891

https://makingmusicmag.com/chord-knowledge/

https://takelessons.com/blog/piano-technique-mistakes-z06

https://www.hoffmanacademy.com/blog/read-chord-symbols-piano/

https://www.britannica.com/art/piano

https://en.wikipedia.org/wiki/Piano

https://colorinmypiano.com/2010/03/02/12-tips-for-memorizing-piano-music/

https://bestdigitalpianoguides.com/piano-chords-and-melodies/

https://www.dummies.com/art-center/music/piano/great-left-hand-accompaniment-patterns-for-the-piano-or-keyboard/

http://www.zebrakeys.com/lessons/beginner/musictheory/?id=12

Piano Music Theory

Swiftly Learn The Piano & Music Theory Essentials and Save Big on Months of Private Lessons! Chords, Intervals, Scales, Songwriting & More.

Tommy Swindali

Table of Contents

Introduction

When making the decision to start learning to play music, specifically that of the piano and/or keyboard, we tend to not know where the best point is to begin. We may be told that YouTube videos are the best place to begin, or that books provide more detail. However, books are too text-heavy, with not enough visual images and diagrams. We tend to forget that many people are visual learners, leading to a quicker learning process when diagrams are included. Music books that are text-heavy are too complex for beginners, as well as being too mundane for the experienced. They lack the presence of lesson plans, which hold a novice musician accountable for their progress. Often, explanations are not included in text-heavy books, leading to a bout of confusion being established that harbors the ability to fully grasp the music knowledge, as well as to progress as a musician.

Music theory forms the foundation of learning to read, understanding and writing music. Once you have established a baseline with the ability to read music, you will be one step closer to playing scales, building chords, and being able to understand key signatures. When we look at this foundation, it primarily encompasses notes, rests, and beats. These basic elements are put together to establish a given rhythm, where the combination of these elements leads to reading, playing and studying music more effectively. As you progress through your musical training, you will start to manipulate and combine notes together into melodic and harmonic compound intervals. You will then be able to focus on establishing compound intervals on a melodic and harmonic scale.

Don't worry; by the end of this book, you will be well acquainted with these terms, as well as be able to successfully link music notation to the positioning of keyboard and/or piano keys. As you start to become more acquainted with music and its notation, you will start to develop a hunger for more in-depth knowledge. Music theory allows you to analyze the ins and outs of music, how the notes are strung together, as well as the best approach towards learning and understanding notation and key signatures. It is because of this that reading music remains an absolute necessity. This is primarily because without being able to read music, the ability to learn songs, songwriting, as well as the foundation of understanding where common errors occur, becomes hindered. This is why it is an absolute necessity to learn the key notations and strategies to read the music notation effectively, accurately, and with minimal mistakes. Music establishes a form of communication that enables you to connect with your listeners - to tell a story. A sense of inspiration also accompanies learning the theory of music. There is a thrill and feeling of complete satisfaction when you are able to build your first song, as well as when you do the first complete playthrough of your favorite classical piece. Music brings people together - friends, family, and even strangers.

Many who want to start learning more about music, automatically have the notion that the task that lies ahead of them is a daunting one. This makes the thought of giving up a lot more favorable than one would think. However, many discount the effectiveness of images and diagrams in learning music. When you are able to link the text to an image, not only are you able to remember the concept better, you are also enabling yourself to establish diagrammatical links (whether it be through a circle or a flow chart) between concepts, further enhancing your own understanding. What one typically finds is that images have the potential to trigger emotions, which makes remembering a concept that much easier.

This book is going to use a combination of text and images in order to enhance the reader's understanding. This book will use a bottom-up approach that focuses on building that strong foundation before moving onto more difficult concepts. This book should be used as a resource, for those new to music as a consistent learning source, and for those experienced in music as more of a refresher. With that being said, this book's author, Tommy Swandili, is an experienced producer and musician who has already made a name for himself through the other music-based publications he has created on Amazon.

The benefits of using this book rather than typical text-heavy books, is that this book will explain concepts using basic English, eliminating the jargon that causes confusion, especially for new musicians. In this book you will learn the exact techniques and strategies needed to learn the keyboard and/or piano efficiently, saving you quite a bit of money on private lessons. By the time you reach the end of this book, you should be able to understand the core concepts of playing music, reading music, composing music, and even being able to write your own songs. The information in this book focuses on a practical and straightforward approach that will definitely help you become a better musician.

Since about 90% of the information that our brains process is visual, it only takes 13 milliseconds for an image to be successfully processed by the human brain. By looking at an image after reading text from the same subject, understanding and interpreting the information becomes easier and will help you establish a strong foundation on which to build your music knowledge.

This book will enrich your current understanding of music, as well as establish a yearning towards wanting to learn more. Now is the time for you to start on your music journey. If not now, when? You are capable of understanding the essence of what music has to offer; and who wouldn't like to be able to whip out a piece of sheet music and start playing their favorite songs? With this book, you can, and you will become an even better keyboard and/or piano player. Your journey towards music success starts here.

Chapter 1: Music Theory Fundamentals

A standard, modern piano has a row of 88 black and white keys. 52 of these keys are white, consisting of notes for the C major scale. 36 of the keys are black keys, raised above the white keys. Some keyboards and pianos come with 66, 72, or 88 keys, which are divided into octaves of eight keys each. These keys are typically described using the C major scale - taking the eight keys from C on one octave, up to another C scale on another octave. The typical manner in which a C major scale will be performed includes the sequential usage of the following keys: C, D, E, F, G, A, B, C.

Before we take a further look into how these notes are arranged, as well as what additions can occur, we will look at some definitions that are essential to understanding music. They are as follows:

- Sound: Musical sounds refer to a regular pattern of vibrations that enter into your ear from an external source (an instrument, song, or crashing sound). As this vibration reaches our ears, internal organs then detect a specific frequency of the vibrations, sending them to the brain to allow us to perceive them as the pitch of a musical tone.
- Pitch: Refers to a specific property of music that occurs based on the rapidity of the vibrations oscillating from the external source of sound. This means that a higher pitch will be defined as more frequently oscillating vibrations that are regular. The contrast is therefore true for a lower pitch, where there are larger intervals present between each oscillation.
- Note: A note is typically that of a single musical sound. There are different types of notes that have differing lengths of

sound production. These can be classified as a semiquaver, quaver, crotchet, minum or semibreve.

• Timbre: The augmentation of music's tone, also known as tone quality, is the perceived sound quality that is perceived when listening to a musical note.

• Tone: An arrangement of pitch, quality and strength that is presented as a heard sound. It is important to note that there are different types of tones that are synonymous with different types of music genres. This becomes a pivotal point in understanding a specific music genre, or alternatively when you write music for a specific genre.

The notes in music are placed on a 'staff.' The staff in music consists of five solid lines with four spaces. When we find a note on each of these lines, or sitting in a specific space, they will represent a different note. The notes A-G move up the staff alphabetically. When we look at the distance between two different musical notes, we can define this as a music interval. In order to better understand what an interval constitutes, it is a whole step and a half step. With a whole step, you are simply moving up one note, thus you are moving from a space between two lines of the staff, onto the line itself (the reverse is also true for this). An example of a whole step would be moving from a C to a D. A half step, on the other hand, is moving between sharps and flats of specific notes; an example of this would be moving from C to C#. Making reference to a piano and/or keyboard, a half step would be moving from a white key to a black key (and vice versa), whereas a whole step would be moving from a white key to another white key, or from a black key to another black key. Intervals are numbered according to the amount of notes that are jumped in order for your initial note to get to your final note. To put this into perspective, if we were to move from a C to an E it would be a third interval as there would have been three steps taken.

When looking at the concept of what a root note is, it is simply just the first note that is present in a chord or scale. This means that if we were to look at the C major scale, the root note would be that of C.

There are two different types of clefs that are pertinent to understanding music notation. These clefs are the treble clef and the bass clef. The treble clef is seen as an ornamental 'G' shape, and is typically present on the left side of the staff. The treble clef characteristically refers to the upper registers of music. This means that instruments that utilize the higher registers, much like that of the flute and saxophone, will primarily have a treble clef written on the sheet music. When we are learning about the bass clef, we are primarily referring to the lower registers of music, such as those that use a lower pitch. Examples of instruments that use a bass clef are the tuba or cello. When we refer the treble and the bass clef in terms of the piano and/or keyboard, both are included. This is primarily because of the higher and lower ranges that can be played on the piano and/or keyboard.

Music is primarily created by combining the concepts of rhythm, melody, and harmony. It should be noted that specific forms of music are characteristically focused on only one or two of these domains, rather than always including all three. An example of this is African drum music that focuses purely on the rhythmic domain. Referring to rhythm, it is the regular patterns of sounds or pitches, enabling us to differentiate between music and noise. Melody refers to the combination of pitch and rhythm. Collectively, these are referred to as the tune, voice, or line, primarily stipulated as the linear succession of musical tones, grouped together in order to allow us to hear a single entity or sound. Harmony then refers to the vertical element of music, where a different amount of notes are played simultaneously on one instrument, or on other instruments. Harmony is also termed 'chords' in music.

When we look at key signatures, they are typically present at the beginning of the first staff, and to the right of the clef. Key signatures remind us as musicians, whether to play the notes in a sharp or a flat. Some keys within the range of keys on the piano and/or keyboard have sharps and flats, which are depicted by the black keys. In some cases where the key signature is not present on at the beginning of the staff, the individual notes themselves will have either a sharp (#) or a flat (♭) signature attached to them. It is the sharp or flat that will inform you of what register the musical piece should be played in.

As we delve into more detailed aspects of music theory, you will start to learn some tricks and mnemonics that help us remember and understand music theory more effectively. Examples of these can be the comparison between the treble clef and the bass clef. The treble clef, which provides us with the higher registers of music, consists of varying note names for the lines and spaces of the staff. Starting on the bottom line of the staff with an E, the space above it would be the next note (F), followed by the next line being a G. Thus, we can break down what note fits onto the staff using the following mnemonics:

• Notes EGBDF: These notes represent those that fall on the line of the staff, starting from the bottom line. An easy mnemonic to remember here would be, 'Every Good Boy Does Fine'.
• Notes FACE: These notes represent the spaces between two lines. With the first space being that at the bottom between notes E and G, the note that will sit here is F. The ascending spaces from there will then follow the 'FACE' mnemonic, until no more spaces are bound by the lines of the staff.'

The treble clef, however, is different from the bass clef, not only in the way it looks, but also in the arrangement of the notes on the staff in order to cater to the lower registers. When we are approached with a bass clef, it is almost as if a lower note is present in the same place as that of the treble clef's higher registers. To explain this better, we shall utilize the following mnemonics:

- Notes GBDFA: These notes represent those that fall on the line of the staff, beginning from the bottom line. The mnemonic to remember here is, 'Good Boys Do Fine Always'. It is important to establish that the notes will increase in an ascending manner.

- Notes ACEG: These notes are present in the spaces between two lines. The first space is present at the bottom of the staff, between notes G and B. The note that will be found here is A. As the notes ascend in spaces, 'All Cows Eat Grass' is the mnemonic that should be followed.

Chapter 2: Scales, Modes and Keys

When we delve a bit deeper into the analysis of music theory, we are required to analyze scales next. A scale is seen as a set of musical notes that are ordered together on the basis of similar frequency (or pitch). There are two main ranges of scales, referring to those that contain an ascending pitch, and contrastingly, those that have a descending pitch. These are termed ascending scales and descending scales respectively.

When we are talking about a scale, musically, we refer to each note of the scale as a particular degree. Along with this degree, comes a specific name. These names allow us to accurately determine which part of a scale is being referred to, saving time and maximizing the performance of the musician. These degrees along with their related names are as follows:

• The first degree (i.e. first note of the scale) is called the 'tonic'.
• The second degree (i.e second note of the scale) is called the 'supertonic'.
• The third degree (i.e third note of the scale) is called the 'mediant'.
• The fourth degree (i.e. fourth note of the scale) is called the 'subdominant'.
• The fifth degree (i.e. fifth note of the scale) is called the 'dominant'.
• The sixth degree (i.e. sixth note of the scale) is called the 'submediant'.
• The seventh degree (i.e. seventh note of the scale) is called the 'leading note'.

At this point you may be asking where the eighth degree is, as an octave has eight notes. Well, the eighth degree of a scale signifies the movement towards a higher octave, directly relating to the tonic of the higher octave. Another manner in which this can be conceptualized is by understanding that there are seven notes between each octave, thus, there can only be up to seven degrees before a higher octave is reached.

There are quite a number of scales that are present within music theory. The good news is that you will not need to learn all the different types at the beginning of your music career. We will primarily be looking at the major, minor and chromatic scales. However, in order to provide you a more holistic view on music theory, there are some scales that are present based on the amount of notes played within the scale. These are classically referred to scales that have a specific amount of different pitch classes in them. For example, the chromatic scale (which will be discussed in more detail later on) consists of 12 notes present per octave. A few other examples of scales are as follows:

•   Pentatonic scale: Consists of five notes per octave, primarily focused on being an anhemitonic form. What this means is that there are no semitones (half step) present. This form of scale is typically seen in folk music, as well as that of many forms of traditional Asian music.
•   Hexatonic scale: Consists of six notes per octave and is commonly found in folk music that is found in Western areas.
•   Heptatonic Scale: Consists of seven notes per octave, and is seen as being the most common scale in use within modern Western music.
•   Octatonic scale: Consists of eight notes per octave and is specifically used in the sheet music of jazz, as well as classical music that is more associated with the modern era.

The Difference Between Major And Minor Scales

The most common scales that we will be using when we learn music notation are the major and minor scales. However, learning them as single entities will help you understand each subject with more ease. It is resoundingly more difficult when needing to incorporate both major and minor scales into your songwriting, as well as when reading music. In order to understand these scales effectively, it is important to reiterate that a semitone refers to a half step, and a tone refers to a whole step.

The Major Scale

The major scale is a very common form of scale that is widely used within the music domain. How we define a major scale, is primarily by the sequence of semitones and tones (i.e. half steps and whole steps) that are present. Remember that there will only be seven degrees within a scale, hence the major scale is only made up of seven notes, with the eighth note leading into the next scale. This can be very confusing at the beginning, so we recommend spending adequate time on solidifying this concept. Thus, a typical combination for that of a major scale would be Tone - Tone - Semitone - Tone - Tone - Tone - Semitone. If we were to alter this to fit the half steps and whole steps dynamic, the above would be Whole step - Whole step - Half step - Whole step - Whole step - Whole step - Half step. This is seen as the common formula, where starting on any note will create a major scale.

Let's try and build some scales together in order to drive the point home. We will start off with the C major scale which typically consists of C, D, E, F, G, A, B, C. The C major scale can therefore be constructed using the following steps:

• The starting note for the C major scale is the C.

- From the C, one will then take a whole step (or move a tone) to D.
- Another whole step is then taken from the D to the E.
- Following the major scale formula, a half step is now taken from E to F.
- A whole step is then taken from F to G.
- A further whole step is taken in order to move from G to A.
- The last whole step for the C major scale will be from A to B.
- To end off the C major scale, the final half step is then taken, taking us from B and returning to C, but an octave higher.

Let's take the creation of scales a bit further, as we focus on a scale that is different from your typical C major scale. We will do this in order to ascertain whether you have fully grasped the concepts of a major scale. The scale that we will learn now will be the D major scale. Note as you are going through this scale, that the D major scale consists of two sharp notes, with the primary notes featured in this scale being D, E, F#, G, A, B, C#, D. The building of this scale is as follows:

- Because we are dealing with the D major scale, the beginning note will be a D.
- The first whole step that will be taken will be from D to E.
- The second whole step in the major scale formula causes the movement from the E to F#.
- We then take a half step from the F# to G.
- Two subsequent whole steps will take us from G to A, and then from A to B.
- A whole step from B will result in a C#.

- Finally, to complete the D major scale, the final half step will return us to D, but an octave higher.

To ensure that the entire concept of a major scale is well understood, the final major scale that we will look at is one with a key signature. This scale will be the E♭ major scale. While building this scale, it is important to note that there are three flats in this scale (the E♭ is only counted once) and that the sequence of notes are E♭, F, G, A♭, B♭, C, D, E♭. The sequence followed to create this scale is as follows:

- The starting note of this scale will be E♭.
- A whole step is then taken to move from E♭ to F.
- The second whole step of the major scale is taken to move F to G.
- A half step then takes us from G to A♭.
- The subsequent three whole steps will then take us from A♭ to B♭, from B♭ to C, and from C to D, respectively.
- The final half step then moves from D to E♭, completing the E♭ major scale.

The Minor Scale

Minor scales can be seen as rather tricky, primarily because there are three types of minor scales, namely natural, melodic, and harmonic. Although we will be focusing on the harmonic minor scale, it is important to know information about the other minor scales should you be confronted with them when you are exploring through music. The differentiations between these three minor scales will be based on degree differences. With the natural minor scale, the third, sixth and seventh degrees need to be played at a half step (semitone) lower than what would originally have been present on a major scale. This completely eliminates the presence of any half steps, creating a scale that is completely whole steps. A melodic minor scale consists of a lowered third degree and a raised sixth degree, when compared to a major scale. When we look at the harmonic minor scale, it compares to the major scale by having a lowered third degree, a lowered sixth degree, and a seventh tone that is raised a half step.

A typical natural minor scale needs to be explained in order for the differing degrees to be well understood. When one makes a natural minor scale, the interval pattern that is used is Tone - Semitone - Tone - Tone - Semitone - Tone - Tone. This can also be read as Whole step - Half step - Whole step - Whole step - Half step - Whole step - Whole step.

The only difference with the formula for a natural minor scale, when converting it to a harmonic minor scale, would be the alteration of the seventh degree, raising it by a half step. Let's take a look at some natural minor scales, and then list how it can be changed into a harmonic minor scale. We will start off by constructing an A natural minor scale. An A natural minor scale has no notes with sharps or flats, with its primary sequence of notes being A, B, C, D, E, F, G, A. The method of construction is as follows:

- The natural A minor scale will start with an A.
- A whole step is then taken from A to B.
- A subsequent half step is then taken from B to C.
- Two whole steps are then taken from C to D, and then from D to E.
- The final half step then takes us from E to F.
- The final two whole steps will then take us from F to G, and from G back to A. However, the A will be the beginning (i.e. first degree) of the next octave.
- If we were to alter this into an A harmonic minor scale, the G will then be raised by a half step to A♭.

To create a visual contrast between the natural and harmonic minor scales. We will go through a C natural minor scale, establish the drawing thereof, and then compare it to the converted C harmonic minor scale so that you can visually see how the change in the seventh degree looks. The C natural minor scale consists of three flats, with its typical sequence being C, D, E♭, F, G, A♭, B♭. How this is constructed is as follows:

- The starting note for the C natural minor scale will be a C.
- A whole step is then taken to move from C to D.
- A half step then moves the D to an E♭.
- Two subsequent whole steps are taken to move the E♭ to a F, and the F to a G.
- The final half step then moves the G to an A♭.
- A whole step moves the A♭ to a B♭.

- The final then moves the B♭ to a C that exists as the first degree in another octave.

- A harmonic change is then made to the seventh degree (i.e. seventh note), raising it by a half step.
- The B♭ is then raised by a half step to B.
- The sequence of the C harmonic minor is then C, D, E♭, F, G, A♭, B.

The Chromatic Scale

In comparison to the major and minor scales, the chromatic scale is very simple to understand. In music there are a total of 12 different notes. This scale focuses on all 12 notes present and is used primarily in Western music. What is unique about this scale is that the 12 notes are all semitones, and there are no tones present at all. In other words, the chromatic scale comprises completely out of half steps. A chromatic scale can therefore start at any of the 12 pitches. This means that if there was a chromatic scale that started on a C, by the end of the scale, a total of 12 different notes would have been played. These types of scales were widely used within the era of romantic music creation. Their utilization within the music construct domain can be used as transitional material, or to finalize a piece. Sometimes, chromatic scales are introduced as a glissando (a continuous upwards or downwards slide between two notes).

Modes

Modes are seen as a type of scale, whereby the alteration of a scale's notes results in the transition from a scale to that of a mode. The typical definition of a diatonic mode refers to a stepwise arrangement of a heptatonic scale. This means that the seven natural pitches (in terms of the scale's degrees) are able to form an octave without having altered the original established pattern. However, as soon as this primary pattern is altered, it begins to form a subclassification of the diatonic mode. There are seven main subclassifications of a diatonic mode. The classifications are the Ionian, Dorian, Phrygian, Lydian, Mixolydian, Aeolian and Locrian modes. Pay very close attention to the subtle differences present with the different modes as this will further allow you to grasp more complicated concepts in music later on.

Ionian Mode

An Ionian mode is seen as a very typical form of mode. It is classically represented by a natural diatonic scale that starts from C and ends on C. It can, thus, be related to a C major scale, with it being paramount that the beginning and end both are on a C. To create some sort of context as to where an Ionian mode can be found would be Vivaldi's Mandolin

Concerto in C major, as well as Mozart's Flute and Harp Concerto in C major.

Dorian Mode

With the Dorian mode, it shows a very strong similarity with the natural minor scale. However, what sets this scale apart is the sixth degree. With a Dorian mode, the sixth degree is seen as a major sixth in comparison to the natural minor scale, which would have a minor sixth. The applications of a Dorian mode in the music industry include the song 'Billie Jean' that was sung by Michael Jackson, as well as 'Smoke on the Water' that was sung by Deep Purple.

Phrygian Mode

The Phrygian mode is also similar to the natural minor scale, however, this difference is primarily on the second degree. It is on this note that a minor is present, not a major like that of which is present in the natural minor scale. With the Phrygian mode being the third type of mode, it is also known as the Spanish gypsy scale. The reason for this is due to the resemblance that it poses with the scales characteristically

found in flamenco music. Musical pieces that include a
Phrygian mode include Liszt's Hungarian Rhapsody No.2,
along with Vaughan Williams's Fantasia on a Theme of Thoma
Tallis.

Lydian Mode

A Lydian mode is similar to the Ionian mode. The only difference is that in a Lydian mode, the fourth degree becomes a sharp, providing a rather unique, yet unsettling sound. The sounds created using a Lydian mode are characteristic. It has been employed in Chopin's Mazurka No.15 as well as Ludwig van Beethoven's String Quartet No.15 in A minor.

Mixolydian Mode

The comparison that is created with the Mixolydian mode is to that of the major scale. The differentiating factor between these two is the seventh degree, whereby the Mixolydian mode includes a flattened seventh degree compared to the major scale's seventh degree. The inclusions of this mode in the musical world include the song 'Norwegian Wood' sung by The Beatles, as well as the theme song to the television series, 'Star Trek.'

Aeolian Mode

The Aeolian mode is seen as a typical natural minor scale. There are absolutely no differences between the two, much like how the C to C major scale is directly related to the Ionian mode. The Aeolian mode is very common in songs, and not so much in classical music. Examples of the Aeolian mode are 'All along the Watchtower' sung by Bob Dylan, as well as 'Losing my Religion', by REM.

Locrian Mode

What makes the Locrian mode so unique is that it contains five notes in its scale that exhibit the flattened nature. These flattened notes are also present as a half step. This mode is present in the works of Rachmaninov, as well as in Sibelius's Symphony No.4 in A minor.

Keys

In music, there are quite a large amount of keys present. In this segment, we do not refer to keys as the physical keys that are present on the keyboard and/or piano; we are referring to a major, minor, or enharmonic key. The key is seen as the aspect around which the music revolves. Typically, the major key is based on a major scale. This means that a song played in the key of C major will be directly related to the seven notes that are present in the C major scale, the same way a song written in the key of F major will have its notes focused around the F major scale. A minor key is the complete opposite, whereby if we were to say that a song is played in the key of A♭,

that it would follow the A♭ scale. Seeing as a minor scale has

three categories, the same concept as above would be applied. An enharmonic key is seen as an identical key that is observed when one looks at both the sharp and flat key signatures. Primarily, it is when the enharmonic equivalent consists of the opposite key signature, thus, a specific sharp scale will have an enharmonic equivalent scale that exhibits a flat key signature. In order for you to understand this a bit better, we will provide some examples. Examples of enharmonic keys and their equivalents would be:

- A C# scale which has D♭ as its enharmonic equivalent.
- A D# scale which has E♭ as its enharmonic equivalent.
- A G# scale which has A♭ as its enharmonic equivalent.
- An A# scale which has B♭ as its enharmonic equivalent.

A very interesting key is that of the relative minor key. The reason this specific key is so interesting is that it exhibits the same key signature, but a different first degree (or tonic note). This is different to that of a parallel minor or major key, mainly because a parallel key would have the same first degree compared to that of the differing first degree in the relative minor key. Let us use some examples to solidify the concepts:

- A C♭ major scale will have an A♭ minor key as its relative minor equivalent.
- A G♭ major scale will have an E♭ minor key as its relative minor equivalent.
- A D♭ major scale will have a B♭ minor key as its relative minor equivalent.

The scales, modes, and keys that you have just learned may seem like a lot of information, and for someone just starting out as a musician, it genuinely is. However, this section has been simplified and fine tuned to such an extent that allows for ease of access, should you want to check your understanding as you progress through the rest of this book.

Chapter 3: Chords, Rhythms, And Movement In Music

Chords

As we start to delve deeper into music, we will learn about constructing chords. A chord is typically seen as the combination or layering of different notes and tones that are played at the same time. However, the manner in which these chords are built is dependent on the type of chord to be created. Typically, the components include a triad with that of a perfect fifth. Referring to that of a 'perfect fifth', it does not mean that one will only play a fifth degree, which is a common error that musicians make, especially when they are novice musicians. The perfect fifth refers to the combination of seven consecutive half steps. Thus, there are seven semitones in a perfect fifth. An example of a perfect fifth would be that from C to G. Taking the above into consideration, a major chord will consist of a major third and a perfect fifth; contrastingly, the minor chord will be made up of a minor third and a perfect fifth.

To understand the components of chords, we need to understand the different types of chords that exist. These are primarily dyads, triads, and tetrads. In music, especially for the piano and/or keyboard, a dyad is composed of two notes or pitches that are played simultaneously to create a chord. A typical example of a dyad would be playing C and E at the same time. There is usually an interval which is present with a dryad, as with what is present between C and E. This means that a dyad of C to E would suggest a key of C major, as it consists of two of the three notes that are typically present in a C major triad chord.

A triad is seen as the most common type of chord that is used in music. A triad consists of three notes. These three notes are typically the root note, the third degree, and the fifth degree. Simply put, these are the beginning note, the third note, and the fifth note, which are separated from each other by a third degree interval. This primarily means that each triad contains notes that are separated by a third degree interval (i.e. two notes between each triad component). In order to solidify this bit of knowledge, we can look at the C major triad. The C major triad consists of a C, E, and G. In these three notes, the C is the root note, E is seen as the third degree, with G being the fifth degree. Between the C and E, as well as the E and G, are two notes. This therefore depicts the separation of these notes using a third degree interval.

If we follow the above patterns, the amount of notes are present in a specific chord. There are four notes present in a tetrad. There are different types of tetrads in music, such as, seventh chords. However, that is some pretty advanced information which will be built on as your journey to becoming a musician progresses.

As we know, with scales, they can be composed of chords. This means that the type of chord you play will be dependent on the amount and presence of intervals that are between each note. It is this that we refer to as the quality of the chord. Furthermore, the quality of a chord will have a direct impact of how it sounds when played. Typically, what this can refer to is a direct tap into one's emotions. A major chord may sound rather happy, whereas when one plays a minor chord, they feel sad.

Now that you know about scales and what chords consist of, the next question you may have is how to construct chords when given a scale. This process is a simple one. You would start on the first note of the scale and move up in thirds, meaning that you would be skipping every alternate note. Placing this into musical talk, starting on the first degree, (also known as the root note) including the third and fifth degrees, will provide you with a three-note chord - known as a triad. The same would apply in terms of creating a dryad or tetrad, focusing on the amount of notes being played simultaneously, along with the amount of intervals present between each note. It is important to mention that more than one chord can be created from a single scale. An example of this would be a major scale, which gives rise to seven diatonic chords.

A fantastic manner in order to change registers, or to move notes or chords from one key to another, is to transpose the notes. A transposition is done by changing all the notes or chords from one major scale to another. One example could be a change from C major scale to a D major scale, where all the notes are changed by one whole step, acting as the primary distance between C and D. Looking at the following chord progression being C - F - A♭ - G - F - C, that is in the C major, if we were to transpose this into the key of D major, every note would be moved by one whole step. The result of this transposition would be D - G - B♭ - A - G - D.

Chord inversions can be rather difficult to understand. The primary way to understand this is to revise the regular position of a chord, along with what a root note is. If we are going to look at a C major triad, the normal positioning of the chord is with the root note being present at the bottom. In a triad, there is typically a first and second inversion that can take place. If the third degree of the chord (e.g. E in a C major triad) is at the bottom, this is called a first inversion. If we were to take the fifth degree and move it to the bottom, we would call this a second inversion.

Some individuals, especially when songwriting, will have the option of changing the notes of a specific chord in a way that has the ability to alter the sound that is heard. This process is called 'Chord Voicing.' This means that if we were to voice an F major triad that is present in the root position, the notes can be arranged in any order as long as the F, A, and C are used in the F major scale, with F being the lowest note on the staff. It is noteworthy to mention that during the chord voicing process, one can move between the treble clef and the bass clef, transitioning between the upper and lower registers.

Chord progressions and arpeggios are the next step that we will be adding to your musician repertoire. A chord progression is seen as a series of two or more chords that are being used in the construction of music pieces. In order to show a progression, as well as the transposition between these chord progressions, roman numerals are used. Thus, using these roman numerals shows how a piece of music will unfold as it is being played. Arpeggios are typically a string of notes, consisting of any chord, whereby the notes are played one note at a time. This is in contrast to how notes are typically played, which is in a simultaneous manner. When we do the C major chord in an arpeggio format, it is playing each of those individual keys of the chord, one after each other.

Some chords just sound a lot better when played together, in comparison to others. It is a rule of thumb, that the first degree, fourth degree, and fifth degree notes of a chord will typically sound more pleasing than that of a second degree, third degree, and fifth degree chord. The chords which produce the most pleasing sounds stem from the C major, F major and G major scales. However, it's only when these sounds are played in a rhythmic manner, that they are pleasing to hear.

Rhythm

Rhythm is an important aspect to practice for any aspiring musician. Rhythm becomes important especially when you are playing in a band, or as a part of an orchestra. Having good rhythm enables you to stay in time with a band, allowing you to remain in beat with the rest of the procession. As you begin to start becoming acquainted with differing rhythms, you will develop sight-reading of good rhythms, as well as become able to play a variety of different rhythms by ear. However, this will take a lot of practice and experience to develop. When one understands rhythm, there is a decreased chance of either rushing the beat, or dragging the beat.

In order to understand rhythm, we need to analyze a few definitions and concepts. These are as follows:

• Beat: A beat is seen as a regular pulse that is repetitive in nature, along with a gap duration and speed which has the ability to allow us to count the beats, acknowledge accented musical sounds, as well as to map music towards a standard external beat regulator. An example of a beat regulator is a metronome.

• Bar: When we see vertical lines in the staff, it is indicative of bar lines. It is with this that we are able to group beats together. The manner in which we are able to assess the number of beats that are present in the bar is through the use of time signatures. There are typically three types of bar lines. A single bar line divides the beats, the double barline indicates the end of a section, with the final bar line indicating the end of the music piece.

• Time signatures: A time signature is seen as a part of musical notation that denotes the type of beat, the amount of beats that are present, as well as the number of beats that are present in a bar. Characteristically, one would find the presence of a time signature in the very first bar, after the double bar line. Time signatures are typically given by four beats in a bar. A duplet is when there are two beats in a bar, a triple is when there are three beats in a bar, with a quadruple being a four beat count in a bar.

• Tempo: When we alter the speed of the beats, we are changing the tempo of the piece. The manner in which we increase or decrease tempo is by changing the amount of beats that occur per minute. One can further change the note value to have an effect on the tempo. If one were to change crotchets to minims, the music would be performed at half of its original tempo.

The time signatures are further divided into two main categories, simple and complex. With simple time signatures, there is a single regular beat that is equal to one regular beat count. This means that if one were to see a 4/4 time signature, it would denote four beats taking place within the bar. A 2/4 and a 3/4 would then denote a duplet and triple respectfully. With a compound time signature, it is the incorporation of three beats equal to one regular beat count. Thus, a full simple time signature would be 4/4 , and a compound time signature would either be 6/8, 9/8, or 12/8.

It is now time to pull all of the concepts that you have already learned into creating your own rhythm. Here are a few steps that you can include in order to successfully create your own first rhythm:

• It is important to find a tempo that you feel comfortable with. How musicians tend to come up with their tempo, is by counting out loud. Counting to four would produce a four-beat cycle, establishing s simple time signature.
• When you are able to find your original tempo, you can play around with doubling and quadrupling of the notes to find a repetitive note cycle that you enjoy.
• You can add onto your rhythm manipulation by accenting subdivisions of your rhythm. This adds a sense of uniqueness to your rhythmic creation.
• Chord voicing along with inversions may provide a very distinct yet pleasurable feel to your rhythm, which can be explored in a variety of different ways.

Movement in Music

Timbre and tone are important aspects that enable one to really flourish when doing movement pieces in tandem with music. When we use the timbre to augment the tone's quality, we are able to implement more brisk movements that are more profound, within a specific tone. When we are able to arrange our sounds based on their pitch, quality and strength, we are able to find specific movements and movement styles that complement the sounds and music composed.

When we combine sounds together, they can either result in a consonance or dissonance. A consonant musical sound is typically described as being pleasant and soothing. Thus, sounds which are described as being comfortable, will be classified as being in consonance. Dissonance is when a musical sound is categorized as sharp, unsettling or unnerving, establishing a sense of tension when being heard. When we watch romantic movies, we are more likely to hear consonant sounds, whereby a thriller or horror movie is more likely to have dissonant sounds.

Referring to drama, it is seen as the use of music and sound to express emotions with the aid of action. The effectiveness of a dramatic performance is based on the strength of the bond between movement and sound, establishing a setting that invigorates audiences while allowing the sounds to be heard effectively.

Chapter 4: Songwriting

Songwriting is not as simple as some would think. It requires revision after revision, the scrapping of ideas, and ensuring that the words match the sounds. It is also noteworthy to mention that there is no fixed manner to write a song. There are different routes and methods that may suit some individuals better than others. When you are about to start writing a song, it is always valuable to do some introspection. What is the message or story that you want to tell? This is where you start finding the melody and rhythm that will not only bring your story to life, but allow you to tell this story to your listeners in a way that is clear and easy to understand. Some songwriters find that they enjoy scripting the chorus first, and then finding a story to complement it.

It helps to write about what you know or something that is important to you. It is a lot easier to write about a subject you are passionate about, or a real-life story that happened to you. Try to have a universal message that listeners can relate to. When you are able to bring out the emotion of a song, you are enabling the listeners to feel your raw emotions, and to understand the journey you had in creating this song. It is important to be passionate about your songwriting. Whilst you are constructing your lyrics, you need to ask yourself whether or not you are delivering your desired message through the melody and lyrics that you have chosen.

How do we go about creating a melody that matches our lyrics? When you start creating your melody, start off by choosing a scale. The reason you should start with a scale is that it limits the amount of notes you can plot, ensuring that you don't waste time looking for notes by ear or checking random keys on your piano and/or keyboards to see if one works. Many decide to use a C major pentatonic scale, which contains C, D, E, G and A. Next, focus on creating a rhythmic succession of the notes in your scale, establishing a contour that establishes how your melody will rise, fall, or remain constant. Once you have the melody, you can play around with the sounds you want to hear. This is important as they need to complement each other. Once you have these components, it is time to revisit your contour line, change some notes around if necessary, and start to fill in your sheet music. If you feel that something is out of place, fix it, whether it be adding extra notes, removing notes, or adjusting the length of these notes.

It is important to also know which genre in which you will be writing your song. As we tackle different genres, it is important that we know what type of audience we want to reach, adapting the genre we write in order to reach them effectively. Some of the different genres used in songwriting include pop, country, rock, urban and blues, amongst many others. The selection of the genre is a very important step as some listeners will prefer to listen to specific genres, while completely avoiding others. If you are planning on writing music and songs for a publisher, your genre is pivotal, as it is one of the core criteria, off of which they will base your music.

It is important to understand that your first song is not going to be perfect. The same may be relevant for your one hundredth song. Songwriting is a skill, one that you will become better at the more you practice. Remember, songwriting, much like with writing music, takes revisiting concepts in order to solidify your knowledge. Music is all about trying until you succeed, and using your failures as stepping stones on your journey in becoming the best musician you can be.

Chapter 5: Orders and Circles

Orders and circles significantly add to your musical knowledge. Focusing on orders, we analyze the order of flats and the order of sharps. These are typically the sequence of flats and sharps as they move along scales and the staff. Sharps will typically follow an ascending pattern from F to B, whereas the flats will typically move in the opposite direction of sharps, primarily from B to F.

The circles of fourths and fifths are primarily present to show the relationship between the 12 notes in music. When we look at the circle of fourths, they primarily let you know how many flats there are in each key. Thus, the circle of fourths will move counterclockwise from C major (which correlates with the twelfth hour on a clock). The purpose of the circle of fourths is primarily to learn which notes will turn into flats. The circle of fifths moves from C major in the clockwise direction, letting us know which notes will turn into sharps, as well as the amount of sharps present. When looking at the circle, one will be able to see that a G major scale has one sharp, whereas the contrasting F major has one flat. However, what people have done is combine the circle of fourths and fifths together into one circle, terming it the circle of fifths. The reason that the circle is termed the circle of fifths is because the key signature is separated by the distance that correlates with a fifth interval.

When we start at C major (correlating with the 12th hour on a clock), and move five whole steps up, and add a sharp in the process, the proper amount of sharps for that key are identified.

One needs to become familiar with the order in which we add sharps. This order is F, C, G, D, A, E, B - correlating with the sequence explained above. So when we analyze the key of C, we can see that there are no sharps present. When we take those five steps up, we reach G. In the key of G, we see that there is one sharp present, which has to be an F# based on the order of sharp addition. Therefore, every single time that one moves five steps up, you will add another sharp. This is where the circle of fifths correlates with the movement of five whole steps between major scales.

The circle of fourths, as previously mentioned, tells us the flats that are present in keys. However, the steps are four up instead of five, correlating with the circle of fourths. Starting from C, there are no flats present. However, when we take those first four whole steps up, we reach an F that the circle shows has one flat. If we were to follow the sequence in which we add flats, which is B, E, A, D, G, C, F, we would be able to identify that a F major scale will consist of a B flat. This means that every time one takes four steps up, another flat is added.

It is important to remember that moving left from the C position gives you the degrees of flats present (referring to the circle of fourths), whereas moving right from the C position will give you the degrees of sharps that are present (referring to the circle of fifths).

Conclusion

The strategies that have been covered in this book have allowed you to grasp the concepts that one would typically pay lots of money for in private instruction. We have paved the journey of learning how to play music, read music, write songs, as well as compose your own melodies, chords, and musical pieces to enhance dramatic performances. It is intended to provide a firm grasp on both the text and visual aspects in this book, where we included significant images that are meant to enhance your understanding of the content.

The exact techniques of learning music, as well as its fundamentals, have been placed in a streamlined fashion that allows you to revisit the basics if you ever feel the need to. In this book, we further focused on how to read music, what sheet music looks like, as well as what the different forms of notation mean. We looked at the definitions of pitch, sound, note, timbre and tone, relating them to the concepts of an octave, harmony, melody and rhythm. We even went further to differentiate between the different clefs that are found in music, as well as what this means for their respective note arrangements on the staff.

You were then introduced to scales, their different types, as well as how modes and keys relate to each other in the creation of song. Building on the idea of songwriting, tricks and tips were given to you to enhance your understanding, as well as guide you to where the best place to start writing a song would be. The creation of these songs were then supplemented with the information that was explained about chords, rhythms, and how to link movement to music.

Lastly, we tackled one of the most confusing aspects in music, the circles of fourths and fifths. We found an easy way to read them, what one actually means when they mean the circle of fourths (i.e. the presence of flats anti-clockwise from C), as well as when one refers to the circle of fifths (i.e. the presence of sharps clockwise from C).

Music on its own is difficult to learn, especially when you have no idea where you should start. However, this book has provided you with a simple guide that is informative, accurate, and easy to understand. You must remember that becoming a musician doesn't happen overnight. It requires constant reevaluation of one's skills, knowledge and experience, focusing on the gaps that you don't know and establishing ways to fill these gaps.

You now have the knowledge about key notations and strategies that will enable you to read music with ease. Remember, music establishes a form of communication that enables you to connect with your listeners, as well as other musicians. It is an art that allows you to tell your story in the manner that you see best. We hope that having reached the end of this book, you are left inspired and want to continue learning other aspects of music theory. You now have the thrill, feeling of satisfaction, and confidence in being able to write your first song. Music brings people together, whether it be friends, family, or strangers. It is a worldwide language that couples with personal growth as you start to build your own repertoire of musical skill. You have now learned the basics of what there is to know about musical theory regarding the piano and/or keyboard. There is still so much waiting for you on the path of becoming the best musician you can be.

References

Alexis, C. (2018, November 12). *29 incredible stats that prove the power of visual marketing.* MovableInk. https://movableink.com/blog/29-incredible-stats-that-prove-the-power-of-visual-marketing/

Farrant, D. (2019). *Types of musical scales: A beginner's guide.* Hello Music Theory: Learn Music Theory Online. https://hellomusictheory.com/learn/music-scales-beginners-guide/

Frederick, R. (n.d.). *TIP #5: Write your song in a genre.* Songwriting Tips and Inspiration. https://robinfrederick.com/five-essential-songwriting-tips/tip-5-write-your-song-in-a-genre/#:~:text=Songwriting%2C%20too%2C%20comes%20in%20different

Gateway, M. (2019, August 22). *Music interval - Music theory 101.* Music Gateway. https://www.musicgateway.com/blog/how-to/music-intervals-theory-with-reference-songs

Gutierrez, K. (2019). *Studies confirm the power of visuals in eLearning.* Shiftelearning.Com. https://www.shiftelearning.com/blog/bid/350326/studies-confirm-the-power-of-visuals-in-elearning

Johnson, C. (2019, August 22). *What is rhythm & why is it so important.* Music Gateway. https://www.musicgateway.com/blog/how-to/what-is-rhythm-why-is-it-so-important#:~:text=Importance%20of%20Having%20Good%20Rhythm&text=Having%20a%20good%20rhythm%20enables

Pilhofer, M. (2016). *What is music theory? - Dummies*. Dummies. https://www.dummies.com/art-center/music/what-is-music-theory/

Pouska, A. (2019). *Keys in music | Harmony*. StudyBass. https://www.studybass.com/lessons/harmony/keys-in-music/

Ross, J. (2019, May 4). *How many musical scales are there (the complete guide)*. Joshua Ross. https://joshuarosspiano.com/how-many-musical-scales-are-there/

Team, M. U. (2017, February 14). *Consonance & dissonance in music*. Musical U. https://www.musical-u.com/learn/consonance-dissonance-music/

Team, M. U. (2017, November 30). *About finding chords in scales*. Musical U. https://www.musical-u.com/learn/about-finding-chords-in-scales/#

Team, M. U. (2018, June 12). *Exploring common chord progressions*. Musical U. https://www.musical-u.com/learn/exploring-common-chord-progressions/

Writer, M. C. (2019, October 1). *Tips for beginning songwriters | Songwriting tips*. Music City SongStar. https://musiccitysongstar.com/songwriting-tips-for-beginners/

All images were created using music composition software, primarily Notation, Composer and Canorus. The word edits were then made using Goodnotes on the iPad.

Discover "How to Find Your Sound"

http://musicprod.ontrapages.com/

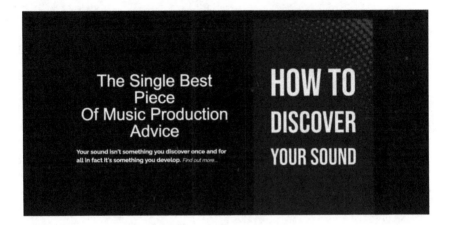

Swindali music coaching/Skype lessons.

Email djswindali@gmail.com for info and pricing

Printed in the USA
CPSIA information can be obtained
at www.ICGtesting.com
LVHW010854211123
764464LV00007BA/113